INTERMITTENT FASTING FOR WOMEN OVER 50

A COMPLETE GUIDE TO REGAIN YOUR BEST SHAPE RESET YOUR METABOLISM AND LOSES WEIGHT

MUJAHID BAKHT

Hardcover: ISBN: 979-8-89302-028-1
Paperback: ISBN: 979-8-89302-027-4
EBook: ISBN: 979-8-89302-029-8

Published by
Atlas Amazon, LLC

United States of America

Copyright © 2024 by Mujahid Bakht

All rights reserved. No part of this book, "Intermittent fasting for women over 50: A Complete Guide to Regain Your Best Shape, Reset Your Metabolism and Lose Weight.", may be reproduced, stored in a retrieval system, or transmitted in any form or by any means, electronic, mechanical, photocopying, recording, or otherwise, without the prior written permission of the publisher, except in the case of brief quotations embodied in critical articles or reviews. For permission requests, write to the publisher, addressed "Attention: Permissions Coordinator," at the following address:

Atlas Amazon, LLC.
244 Fifth Avenue, Suite D210
New York, NY 10001 USA

DISCLAIMER

This book is intended for informational purposes only and is not a substitute for professional medical advice. Readers should consult their healthcare provider before starting any new diet or exercise program, including intermittent fasting. The author and publisher disclaim any liability for any adverse effects that may result from the use of the information in this book. Although every effort has been made to ensure the accuracy of the information, diet and health results can vary greatly by individual. No guarantees are made about the results of following the recommendations contained herein.

TABLE OF CONTENTS

INTRODUCTION 8
- How to Use this eBook 13
- Who This Book Is For 15

CHAPTER 1 19
INTRODUCTION TO INTERMITTENT FASTING 19
- History and Evolution of Fasting 22
- Benefits Specifically for Women Over 50 24
- Hormonal Advantages 24
- Common Myths Debunked 26
- Realities Backed by Science 27
- Safety Guidelines 28

CHAPTER 2 31
CHOOSING YOUR FASTING PLAN 31
- Popular Fasting Methods 31
- OMAD (One Meal a Day) 33
- Customizing Your Fasting Schedule 33
- What to Expect in the First Month 36
- Fasting as a Lifestyle 39
- Integrating Fasting Sustainably into Daily Life 39
- Feedback and Adjustments 41

CHAPTER 3 44
NUTRITION FUNDAMENTALS 44
- Nutritional Needs for Women Over 50 44
- Adjustments for Age-Related Dietary Needs 45
- Eating Strategies during Feeding Windows 46
- Hydration and Intermittent Fasting 49
- Supplements to Consider 52

Avoiding Nutritional Pitfalls 54
How to Overcome Them 56

CHAPTER 4 58

EXERCISE INTEGRATION 58

Benefits of Exercise While Fasting 58
Cardiovascular Exercises 60
Strength Training 63
High-Quality Protein Intake 64
Flexibility and Balance 66
Strength Training with a Focus on Lower Body: 69
Creating a Balanced Routine 116

CHAPTER 5 120

RECIPE BOOK I - BREAKFASTS AND SNACKS 120

Understanding Meal Composition 120
Ideas for Quick and Nutritious Breakfasts 121
Vegetarian Breakfast Recipes 130
Berry Almond Breakfast Bowl 132
Non-Vegetarian Breakfast Recipes 139
Healthy Snacks 148
Low-Calorie Options 152
Beverages 155

CHAPTER 6 159

RECIPE - LUNCHES AND DINNERS 159

Meal Planning Strategies 159
Vegetarian Lunch Recipes 161
Warm, Comforting Soups recipes 164
Non-Vegetarian Lunch Recipes 167
Fish, Poultry, and Meat Dishes 167
Vegetarian Dinner Recipes 171

    Quick Fixes for Busy Nights 174
    Non-Vegetarian Dinner Recipes 177
    Nutrient-Dense Meals to End the Day 178
    Cooking Techniques That Retain Flavor 180

CHAPTER 7 .... **182**
OVERCOMING CHALLENGES AND PLATEAUS **182**
    Managing Hunger Pangs 182
    Dealing with Weight Plateaus 184
    Understanding Weight Plateaus 185
    Emotional and Psychological Aspects 187
    Managing Mood Swings 187
    Adapting Fasting for Health Issues 189
    Fasting During Special Occasions 193

CHAPTER 8 .... **196**
ADVANCED FASTING TECHNIQUES **196**
    Periodic Prolonged Fasting 196
    Autophagy and Its Benefits 199
    Combining Fasting With Keto 201
    Fasting Mimicking Diets 204
    Troubleshooting Common Issues 207

CHAPTER 9 .... **210**
SUSTAINING YOUR NEW LIFESTYLE **210**
    Maintaining Intermittent Fasting Long-Term 210
    Continued Learning and Adaptation 212
    Integrating Mindfulness and Meditation 214
    Fasting and Global Traditions 217
    Looking Ahead 219

Appendix **222**

ABOUT AUTHOR

MR. MUJAHID BAKHT:-

LIFE HISTORY:- Mr. Bakht is a mature, experienced administrator with thirty-seven years of experience as a businessman in international marketing and public relations. Mr. Bakht is an International Real Estate Specialist, and Professional Business and Projects Consultant. He was born in Pakistan and educated in Pakistan and the USA. Presently American Citizen belongs to a business-oriented family—thirty-seven years Resident of New York, USA.

BUSINESS HISTORY:- Mr. Bakht is a Founder and President of Atlas Amazon, LLC., Mr. Bakht is a business developer and multilingual business specialist in the Caribbean, South East Asia, and the Middle East emerging markets Mr. Bakht has served, met, and hosted many "Heads of the Countries" Also, maintain a close relationship with investors of high net worth in the USA.

CAREER:- Mr. Bakht has been engaged with many multinational companies in the field of international real estate investment, communication, technology, diamond, gold, mining, Pre-Feb housing, wind & solar energy, outsourcing management, and project consulting along with business partners & associates worldwide. Mr. Bakht has participated in major national and international conferences including participated in United Nations (U.N.O.) conferences.

TRAVEL:- Mr. Bakht is well-traveled and has visited many countries worldwide.

MANAGEMENT EXPERIENCE:- Thirty-seven years of diversified experience in project consulting, marketing, and business management. As a Director of Marketing, Director of

Public Relations, Director of International Affairs, Executive Vice President, President, CEO, and Chairman of many national & multinational companies, where he served previously. Mr. Bakht hired and trained many professionals as business consultants in international marketing and supervised them. Mr. Bakht is the author and publisher of multiple books.

PERSONAL HISTORY:- Mr. Bakht married in 1992 in New York City, USA. He is a Father of three children, all three were Born raised, and educated in the United States of America.

Dartmouth College, New Hampshire, USA.
St. John University, Queens, New York, USA.
Syracuse University, Upstate New York, USA.

CERTIFICATES; Certificate of Authenticity from Bill Rodham Clinton, President of the United States, and Hillary Rodham Clinton First Lady, USA. (July 20, 2000);

HONORS MEMBER; Madison Who's Who of Professionals, having demonstrated exemplary achievement and distinguished contributions to the business community, registered at the Library of Congress in Washington D.C. USA. (2007 & 2008)

HONORS MEMBER; Premiere Who's Who International, professional business executive having demonstrated exemplary achievement and distinguished contributions to the International business community, 2008 - 2009.

CERTIFICATE OF ACHIEVEMENT; The Achievement Award was presented to Mr. Bakht by Stephen Fossler for five years of continued growth and customer satisfaction from 1996 to 2001.
CERTIFICATE OF AUTHENTICITY; from Terence R. McAuliffe, Chairman of Democratic National Committee, Tom Dachle, Senate Democratic Leader, Dick Gephardt, House

Democratic Leader, USA. (June 16, 2001);

CERTIFICATE OF AUTHENTICITY; from Terence R. McAuliffe, Chairman of Democratic National Committee, USA. (April 16, 2002).

MEETINGS WITH DIGNITARIES AND HEADS OF THE COUNTRIES:

Honorable. Teng-Hui-Lee, President of Taiwan. 1999.
Hon. Leonard Fernandez, President of the Dominican Republic. 1999.
Prince. Ahmed Fahad Al-Turki, (Saudi Arabia). 2000.
Benazir Bhutto, Prime Minister of Pakistan, 2001.
Dr. Keith Mitchell, Prime Minister of Grenada, West Indies. 2003-2004.
Pierre Charles, Prime Minister of Dominica, West Indies, 2003.
Mr. Charles Sovran, Foreign Minister of Dominica, 2003.
Robert H. O. Corbin Leader & Deputy-Prime-Minister (PNC) Guyana 2004.
Hon. P. J. Peterson, Prime Minister of Jamaica. 2004.
Dr. Kenny D. Anthony, Prime Minister of Saint Lucia, West Indies. 2005.
Hon. Owen Arthur, Prime Minister of Barbados, West Indies. 2005.
Michael de la Bastide, "Chief Justice" and President of the Caribbean Islands. 2005.
Mahmood M. Hussain, the Private Office of His Royal Highness. Dr. Sheikh-
Sultan Bin Khalifa Bin Zayed Al Nahyan, Abu-Dhabi, U.A.E. 2005.
Sultan S. Al Mansoori, Saeed & Mohammed Alnaboodah, Dubai, UAE 2005.
Ibrahim A. Gambari, Under-Secretary-General (United Nations) 2006.

Hon. Villasarao Deshmukh, Chief Minister of Maharashtra, India, 2006.
Hon. Ashok Chovan, Minister of Industries, Maharashtra, India, 2006.
Hon. Liu Bowie, Ambassador of China, United Nations, 2006.
Senator Einstein Louison, Ministry of Agriculture, Grenada.
Hon. Mark Isaac, Minister of State, Grenada, West Indies.
Hon. Brenda Hood, Minister for Tourism, Civil Aviation, Culture, Grenada.
Wayne Smith, Mayor, Township of Irvington, New Jersey, USA.
Orlando J. Moreno, Brigadier General & Military Advisor, (UNO) Venezuela.

INTRODUCTION

Welcome to "Intermittent Fasting for Women over 50," a comprehensive guide designed to empower you with a transformative approach to health and wellness through intermittent fasting. This book is tailored specifically for women over 50, addressing unique nutritional needs and health considerations with precise and thoughtful strategies.

This book endeavors to serve as your mentor on a journey towards revitalized health and well-being. Intermittent fasting is not just a dietary choice; it's a lifestyle decision that can significantly impact various aspects of health, from metabolic rate to hormonal balance. We aim to demystify intermittent fasting for you, outlining not only the science behind it but also the practical aspects of integrating it seamlessly into your life.

You can expect this book to cover a range of crucial topics. We begin with the fundamentals of intermittent fasting, explaining its principles and various methods that can be adapted to fit your lifestyle and health status. From there, we will guide you through nutritional strategies, providing over 100 delicious recipes that cater to both vegetarian and non-vegetarian diets, ensuring you maintain a balanced and fulfilling diet.

Exercise, often a daunting aspect for many in this age group, will be addressed comprehensively. We provide detailed exercise plans that enhance the efficacy of fasting without compromising your energy levels or health. Moreover, this book will not shy away from the challenges and plateaus commonly faced; instead, it will equip you with strategies to overcome them, ensuring your fasting journey is successful and sustainable.

This guide will offer insights into the psychological and emotional facets of adopting a new eating pattern, which is often overlooked in other texts. We aim to support your mental and emotional well-being by providing real-life testimonials and motivational stories to inspire and guide you.

How to Use this eBook

To get the most out of this eBook, start by reading through each chapter sequentially. Each section builds on the last, gradually enhancing your understanding and readiness to begin intermittent fasting. Take the time to absorb the information, and keep a journal of your thoughts and plans for how you might integrate these changes into your life.

Navigating the contents is straightforward: each chapter is designed to stand alone, allowing you to return to specific sections easily as you deepen your practice of intermittent fasting. We have included detailed tables of contents and indexes to help you quickly find information as needed.

Practical tips are scattered throughout the book to aid your journey. These include sidebars on troubleshooting common issues, adapting the fasting plan to your needs, and maintaining your new lifestyle in the long term. We also encourage you to engage with the interactive elements, such as reflection prompts and quizzes, designed to facilitate deeper understanding and personalization of the content.

As you progress through this book, each chapter will specifically address the aspects of intermittent fasting that best suit the needs of women over 50. This isn't just a diet book; it is a holistic health resource focusing on longevity and quality of life. Here's how you can fully engage with and benefit from each part of the content provided.

Embracing the Lifestyle

Intermittent fasting offers more than just a method to lose weight—it provides a pathway to rediscover your body's natural rhythms and optimize them for better health and increased vitality. As you read, remember that the process is highly individual. What works well for one person might need adjustment for another. This book teaches you how to listen to your body and modify your fasting plans as your needs evolve, especially during the later stages of life when such attentiveness becomes all the more critical.

Cultivating Patience and Consistency

Patience is key when adapting to any new lifestyle change, especially one as significant as intermittent fasting. Initial results might not be instantaneous, and this is perfectly normal. This guide will help you set realistic expectations, measure progress in ways that go beyond the scale, and stay motivated. Consistency in following the fasting methods and dietary advice provided here is crucial; however, flexibility is equally important to ensure that the plan remains practical and sustainable in the long term.

Leveraging Community and Support

While the journey of intermittent fasting is personal, community support can play a vital role in maintaining motivation and providing accountability. This book includes sections on building a support network, whether through online communities, local groups, or with friends and family who are also exploring fasting lifestyles. Sharing experiences and challenges not only helps to normalize the struggles but also celebrates the milestones achieved along the way.

Advanced Topics for Deeper Understanding

For those who find themselves fascinated by the science of fasting or wish to delve deeper into its mechanisms, advanced topics are covered in the latter chapters. These sections include discussions on autophagy, the process by which your body cleanses damaged cells; how fasting impacts cellular repair and regeneration; and the integration of fasting with other dietary approaches like the ketogenic diet for enhanced effects.

Continuous Learning and Adaptation

This guide is designed not just to educate but also to inspire ongoing learning and adaptation. As research on intermittent fasting continues to evolve, so too should your practices. We provide a comprehensive list of resources for further reading—scientific studies, books, and articles—that can help you stay informed about the latest discoveries and methodologies.

Mindfulness and Emotional Well-being

Integrating mindfulness into your fasting routine can enhance the benefits of intermittent fasting by improving your stress response and emotional well-being. Techniques such as meditation, guided breathing, and yoga are recommended to complement your dietary practice, helping to center your mind and reduce the emotional challenges associated with dietary changes.

Who This Book Is For

Intermittent Fasting for Women Over 50" is meticulously crafted for women who are navigating the complex transition of midlife and seeking ways to enhance their health and vitality through informed dietary strategies. This book recognizes the unique challenges faced by women in this age group, particularly the shifts in metabolic rate, hormonal changes, and lifestyle adjustments that accompany ageing. It is designed not just as a guide but as a companion to help you embrace a lifestyle that fosters health, emotional well-being, and a renewed sense of energy.

The primary audience for this book is women over the age of 50 who are either contemplating or already practising intermittent fasting. This period in life is often marked by significant physiological changes, including menopause and its associated symptoms like weight gain, decreased bone density, and shifts in blood sugar levels. Many women find that the dietary and exercise routines that worked for them in their thirties and forties are no longer effective as they enter their fifties and beyond. This book provides the insights and adaptations necessary to tailor intermittent fasting methods to their evolving needs.

Women at this stage are also likely dealing with various life transitions, including changes in career, family dynamics, and personal relationships. Such changes can bring about stress, which in turn can influence eating habits and overall health. This guide offers not only dietary advice but also strategies to manage stress and maintain mental and physical health through these transitions.

This demographic often includes grandmothers, mothers, community leaders, and business professionals who balance multiple responsibilities. They need a program that is flexible, adaptable, and simple enough to integrate into a busy and sometimes unpredictable life. This book addresses these requirements by providing practical tips for personalizing the intermittent fasting lifestyle to fit varied daily routines and commitments.

Personalization Tips

1. Starting Slowly: One key piece of advice offered in this book is to start the intermittent fasting journey slowly. For women over 50, especially those who are new to fasting, it is important to gradually ease into fasting schedules to reduce shock to the body and to learn how their bodies react to different fasting windows. This could mean starting with a modest 12-hour overnight fast and slowly building up to more restrictive patterns as comfort and confidence grow.

2. Listening to Your Body: As women age, they often experience an increased sensitivity to diet and exercise changes. This book teaches readers to listen carefully to their bodies. Signs of fatigue, irritability, or other discomforts can be indicators that adjustments are needed in the fasting schedule or nutritional intake. Personalization means adapting the guidance in this book to fit personal health indicators and comfort levels.

3. Adjusting for Physical Activity: The level of physical activity plays a critical role in how the fasting schedule should be structured. Active women may require more substantial feeding windows or more frequent protein-rich meals to support their energy needs. This book provides several model schedules that can be adjusted based on workout intensity and timing, ensuring that readers can maintain their physical activity without compromising their nutritional health.

4. Integrating Medical Advice: Intermittent fasting can still be beneficial for those with health conditions like diabetes, thyroid issues, or high blood pressure, but it must be approached more cautiously. This guide emphasizes the importance of consulting healthcare providers to tailor the fasting approach to work synergistically with medical treatments and dietary needs prescribed for underlying health conditions.

5. Embracing Mindfulness and Emotional Health: Mental health is profoundly linked to physical health, especially for fasting regimens. Stress can sabotage fasting benefits by influencing hormonal balances like cortisol levels, which affect fat storage and hunger. Meditation, mindful eating, and cognitive behavioural strategies are discussed as methods to enhance the emotional benefits of intermittent fasting.

6. Community Engagement: Lastly, finding or creating a community of like-minded individuals who are also exploring intermittent fasting can enhance the experience. This book suggests ways to connect with others through online forums, local groups, or even friends and family. Sharing experiences, challenges, and successes can provide support and motivation, which are crucial for maintaining long-term adherence to a fasting plan.

CHAPTER 1
INTRODUCTION TO INTERMITTENT FASTING

An eating schedule that alternates between eating and fasting is called intermittent fasting. Intermittent fasting centers on when you eat, as opposed to diet regimens that emphasize what you consume. It organizes your daily eating schedule into times when you are allowed to eat (feeding windows) and times when you are not (fasting periods). This approach does not necessarily change your diet but restructures you're eating pattern to reap various health benefits.

This method has been around for centuries, often embedded in cultural and religious practices worldwide. Only recently has it gained significant attention from the health community and the public for its potential to improve longevity, brain health, and metabolic efficiency.

The core idea behind intermittent fasting is to allow the body time to exhaust its sugar stores and start burning fat. Normally, the body relies on carbohydrates from food for energy. When you fast, the body gradually runs out of this quick fuel source and begins to tap into fat reserves for energy, a process known as metabolic switching. This switch not only aids in weight loss but also improves metabolic health.

There are several popular methods of intermittent fasting, each varying by fasting times and frequency. Some fast for 16 hours a day, while others fast for a full 24 hours o nce or twice a week. No matter the method, the fundamental principle remains the same: strategically alternating eating and fasting periods to improve health.

Intermittent fasting offers particular benefits for women over 50. It can help manage weight, improve insulin sensitivity, and reduce inflammation—factors that are crucial as the body ages. Additionally intermittent fasting has been connected to enhanced mental performance and a lower risk of neurodegenerative diseases.

The practice not only encourages physiological changes but also fosters a new relationship with food. It teaches restraint and mindfulness, which can lead to more thoughtful eating habits and improved dietary choices. Over time, practitioners often find that they naturally start to prefer more nutritious foods and smaller portions, which contribute to better health. As straightforward as it sounds, intermittent fasting is a profound tool for health enhancement.

It is a flexible method for people who want to enhance their health via dietary modifications since it can be adjusted to fit a variety of li festyles and health concerns. The following sections will delve deeper into the different fasting methods, how to determine the best one for you, and how to begin your intermittent fasting journey effectively, ensuring it complements your lifestyle and personal health goals.

By understanding and applying the principles of intermittent fasting, you can take significant steps towards a healthier, more vibrant life. The key is to approach this change thoughtfully and to adapt the general guidelines to your specific circumstances with an emphasis on gradual change and personal comfort.

Intermittent fasting is often described as a cyclic pattern of eating that alternates between designated periods of eating and not eating. This pattern isn't about cutting out specific foods or drastically reducing calorie intake overall but is focused on when you should eat those calories. This time-restricted feeding helps organize your daily or weekly eating schedule into times of food intake and times of fasting.

The scientific principles behind intermittent fasting are rooted in the body's metabolic processes. Insulin is released by the body during feeding to aid in the conversion of dietary carbohydrates into energy. The extra energy is then kept in fat cells. When you go for extended periods without food, your body starts using fat reserves for energy because your insulin levels drop. This process is called fasting.

This fasting state triggers several cellular and molecular mechanisms that benefit your health. One key process is called autophagy, where cells remove damaged components, aiding in cell repair and the regeneration of new cells. This process is crucial for preventing diseases such as cancer, Alzheimer's disease, and heart disease.

Fasting intermittently improves hormone function, which helps with weight loss. More efficient breakdown and use of body fat for energy is facilitated by reduced insulin, increased growth hormone, and elevated norepinephrine levels. This hormonal shift lowers the risk of metabolic disorders including type 2 diabetes by increasing metabolic efficiency and aiding in weight loss.

Intermittent fasting affects gene expression; genes vital for longevity and protection against disease start to function differently. Fasting has been demonstrated in studies to lower oxidative stress, enhance disease biomarkers, and maintain memory and learning abilities. Together, these advantages support increased health and slower aging.

Intermittent fasting makes you not just metabolically efficient but also aids in better health management by aligning your eating pattern with the natural rhythms of your body's metabolism. This synchronization maximizes energy utilization, enhances bodily functions, and prolongs cell health, thereby contributing to longer and healthier living. This concept of timing in eating can dramatically improve your body's ability to function at its best, showing that when you eat can be as important as what you eat.

History and Evolution of Fasting

Fasting, the practice of voluntarily abstaining from food for a specific period, has deep roots in both cultural traditions and historical practices around the world. This ancient practice has been adapted through the ages, evolving into the modern dietary approach known as intermittent fasting.

Cultural and Historical Perspective

Historically, fasting is as old as mankind. Early hunter-gatherer societies experienced fasting unintentionally due to their inconsistent access to food. This not only shaped their eating patterns but also their metabolisms, which adapted to prolonged periods without food. As civilizations advanced, fasting became a structured part of many cultural and religious rituals.

One important aspect of spiritual discipline in many religions is fasting. It is customary for Christians to fast during Lent, Jews celebrate Yom Kippur, and Muslims fast from sunrise to sunset during the month of Ramadan. Self-control, humility, and spiritual development are the goals of these religious activities.

Beyond religion, fasting has been used as a method of political protest or a statement of non-violent resistance. Notable figures such as Mahatma Gandhi fasted to promote peace and social change. In these contexts, fasting underscores the power of passive resistance and the human spirit's capacity to endure hardship for a greater cause.

Evolution into Modern Practices

The transition of fasting from primarily religious and cultural practices to a component of modern health and wellness routines began in the 20th century. As scientific understanding of human biology advanced, researchers began to explore the physiological impacts of fasting beyond its spiritual and psychological benefits.

In the 1930s, scientists began documenting the health benefits related to caloric restriction, including longevity and reduced incidence of diseases. These studies laid the groundwork for developing structured intermittent fasting regimens as a means to enhance health deliberately.

Modern intermittent fasting gained popular momentum in the 21st century with the proliferation of diet trends and increased focus on lifestyle as a component of health care. Medical professionals and health influencers began advocating for intermittent fasting not just as a weight loss technique but as a holistic approach to improving bodily functions, enhancing mental clarity, and prolonging life expectancy.

The 16/8 technique, which involves fasting for 16 hours a day and eating during an 8-hour window, and the 5:2 approach, which calls for five days of normal eating, are two examples of the many ways used today for intermittent fasting.

A week and reducing calorie intake for two non-consecutive days. These methods have been adapted to fit the flexible and diverse lifestyles of modern society, making intermittent fasting a versatile and accessible practice for improving health and wellness.

The evolution of fasting from an involuntary survival strategy to a voluntary health regimen illustrates its significant role in human history and its potential in contemporary health management. As we continue to learn more about human physiology, the practice of fasting remains a poignant reminder of the interconnectedness of culture, history, and biology.

Benefits Specifically for Women Over 50

Intermittent fasting offers a range of health benefits that are particularly advantageous for women over 50. As women enter this stage of life, they face unique health challenges, particularly related to hormonal transitions and metabolic changes. Intermittent fasting can be a strategic tool to alleviate and manage these changes effectively.

Hormonal Advantages

One of the most significant transitions for women over 50 is menopause, during which the body undergoes profound hormonal changes, notably a decline in estrogen levels. This decline is associated with various symptoms such as weight gain, hot flashes, and increased risk of osteoporosis. Intermittent fasting can help mitigate these symptoms through its impact on hormonal balance.

Fasting helps regulate insulin levels in the body. High insulin levels are linked to insulin resistance, a common condition in postmenopausal women that can lead to type 2 diabetes and weight gain. By improving insulin sensitivity, intermittent fasting reduces the risk of developing insulin resistance, helping to stabilize energy levels and curb cravings.

Intermittent fasting can increase human growth hormone (HGH) production, which decreases with age. HGH plays an important part in maintaining muscle mass, improving metabolism, and burning fat. By enhancing HGH levels, fasting not only helps in weight management but also supports healthier ageing, reducing the risk of developing sarcopenia (muscle loss related to ageing).

Metabolic Health Benefits

Women over 50 frequently see a slowing in their metabolism, which can lead to weight gain and increased fat storage, especially in the abdominal area. Intermittent fasting boosts metabolic rate by increasing norepinephrine levels, which assist in fat burning and overall energy expenditure.

This fasting-induced boost in metabolism helps to convert food more efficiently into energy rather than storing it as fat. Additionally, the procedure helps lower inflammation, which is a major contributing factor to a number of chronic illnesses, such as Alzheimer's, arthritis, and heart disease, to which older women are especially vulnerable.

The body uses intermittent fasting to improve cellular repair mechanisms like autophagy, which helps it eliminate damaged cells and replace them with new ones. This is particularly beneficial as the immune system typically weakens with age. Enhanced autophagy can lead to better cellular maintenance and a lower likelihood of age-related diseases.

By integrating intermittent fasting into their lifestyles, women over 50 can gain profound health benefits that go beyond weight management. It offers a pathway to improved hormonal balance, better metabolic health, and enhanced overall vitality, helping them not only extend their lifespan but also improve the quality of their later years. This dietary modification, when combined with regular physical activity and balanced nutrition, can significantly enhance life quality and provide a strong foundation for healthy ageing.

Common Myths Debunked

Intermittent fasting has grown significantly in popularity, but as with many health trends, there are numerous misconceptions surrounding its practice. These myths can deter individuals, especially women over 50, from exploring a potentially beneficial health strategy. Let's clarify these misconceptions and highlight the realities as supported by scientific evidence.

Clarifying Misconceptions

Myth 1: Intermittent Fasting is Just Another Diet Fad

Many people lump intermittent fasting in with transient dietary trends. However, unlike fad diets that focus on what to eliminate from your diet, intermittent fasting is about timing your meals to align with natural metabolic cycles. This practice is not only sustainable but also backed by extensive research indicating its benefits for longevity, metabolic health, and neuroprotection.

Myth 2: Fasting Slows Down Metabolism

A common concern is that fasting might slow down the metabolism, making it harder to lose weight or maintain weight loss. On the other hand, studies have demonstrated that brief fasting raises metabolic rates by as much as 14%. . This increase is due to a rise in norepinephrine, which helps the body burn fat more effectively.

Myth 3: Intermittent Fasting Leads to Overeating

There is a belief that fasting will cause one to overeat during allowed eating periods, negating any caloric deficit created by the fast. Research indicates that although there is an increase in meal size after a fast, overall calorie intake does not rise significantly.

Most people naturally eat less when they eat within a restricted time window.

Myth 4: Intermittent Fasting Causes Muscle Loss

Another myth is that fasting causes the body to consume muscle for fuel, leading to muscle loss. Studies suggest that as long as the fasting is not excessively prolonged, the body primarily burns fat for energy. Furthermore, human growth hormone levels may be greatly raised by intermittent fasting, which is advantageous for the development and maintenance of muscle.

Realities Backed by Science

Reality 1: Fasting Improves Insulin Sensitivity

Among the most significant, scientifically supported advantages of sporadic fasting include the improvement in insulin sensitivity. This effect is crucial for preventing type 2 diabetes, a common concern for women over 50. Better insulin sensitivity means the body can manage blood sugar more effectively, reducing the risk of diabetes.

Reality 2: Fasting Enhances Brain Health

Intermittent fasting boosts the synthesis of the protein brain-derived neurotrophic factor (BDNF), which is essential forneuron health. Increased levels of BDNF have been linked to improved memory, better mood, and a lower danger of neurological conditions like Alzheimer's.

Reality 3: Fasting Promotes Cellular Repair and Autophagy

The body uses autophagy to recycle damaged cells and create new ones. A number of illnesses, such as cancer and Alzheimer's disease, can be avoided by following this approach. Autophagy is triggered by fasting and contributes to the upkeep of cellular health and function.

Reality 4: Fasting Supports Weight Loss and Metabolic Health

Intermittent fasting leads to reduction in weight and improved metabolic health by shifting the body's energy usage from sugars to fats, a process known as metabolic switching. This switch not only helps in reducing body fat but also improves health markers such as blood pressure and cholesterol levels.

Understanding these realities can provide clarity and confidence to women over 50 considering intermittent fasting as a health strategy. With its roots in science and its numerous documented benefits, intermittent fasting stands out as a valuable and sustainable approach to improving health and quality of life in later years. By debunking common myths and highlighting factual benefits, this guide aims to empower women to make informed decisions about incorporating intermittent fasting into their wellness routines.

Safety Guidelines

While intermittent fasting offers numerous health benefits, it is not suitable for everyone. Specific conditions and health scenarios make fasting inappropriate or even dangerous. It is crucial to understand when to avoid fasting and to consider medical advice before starting any new diet regimen, especially one that involves altering your eating schedule significantly.

When to Avoid Fasting

If You Are Underweight

Underweight individuals should not fast. Fasting can exacerbate the risks of malnutrition and other health problems associated with being underweight, such as weakened immunity, osteoporosis, and hormonal imbalances.

If You Have a History of Eating Disorders

Anyone with a current or previous eating disorder should avoid intermittent fasting. Fasting can trigger unhealthy behaviors in susceptible individuals, potentially leading to relapses in conditions like anorexia or bulimia.

If You Are Pregnant or Breastfeeding

Pregnant and breastfeeding women should not engage in intermittent fasting. During these periods, there is an increased demand for nutrition to support the mother's health as well as the baby's growth and development. Fasting could compromise nutrient intake and energy levels, which are critical during pregnancy and lactation.

If You Have Certain Medical Conditions:

People with diabetes, particularly those on insulin or insulin-stimulating medications, should be cautious. Fasting can significantly alter blood sugar levels, requiring careful management under medical supervision. Additionally, individuals with chronic diseases such as heart disease should consult their doctor before starting a fasting regimen.

Medical Considerations

Consult With a Healthcare Provider

See your doctor before starting any intermittent fasting program, especially if you are taking medication or have any chronic health conditions. A healthcare provider can offer guidance based on your health status and medications that may need to be adjusted during fasting.

Monitor Your Health

Pay close attention to how your body reacts when you start intermittent fasting. Common side effects can include fatigue, headaches, and irritability, which typically resolve as the body adjusts. However, if you experience severe symptoms, such as fainting spells, extreme weakness, or other significant health changes, stop fasting and consult a healthcare provider.

Medication Timing and Management

The timing of medication can be crucial, especially for medicines that need to be taken with food. Fasting may require adjustments in the timing and dosage of medication. This is particularly important for blood pressure medications, diabetic medications, and any other treatments that could interact with nutrient intake.

Hydration is Key

Maintaining hydration is essential during fasting periods. Water is crucial, but you may also need to incorporate electrolyte solutions, especially if you're fasting for over 24 hours or are active during fasting periods. Steer clear of dehydration as it might result in major health problems such as urinary tract infections and kidney stones.

Women over 50 can safely get the benefits of intermittent fasting while lowering dangers by following these safety measures. It's important to approach fasting as a part of a holistic health strategy—balancing nutrition, exercise, and regular medical check-ups to maintain overall health and well-being. This careful approach ensures that the fasting experience is positive, health-promoting, and sustainable in the long term.

CHAPTER 2

CHOOSING YOUR FASTING PLAN

Selecting the right intermittent fasting plan is essential to maximizing its health benefits while ensuring it aligns with your lifestyle, current health status, and personal preferences. Here, we explore some of the most popular fasting methods, as well as a few lesser-known options that might suit particular needs better.

Popular Fasting Methods

16/8 Method

This type of intermittent fasting is the most often used and is renowned for being both easy to follow and efficient. The 16/8 technique calls for 16 consecutive hours and limiting your eating to an eight-hours window each day. For many, this means skipping breakfast, consuming their first meal at noon, and finishing dinner by 8 PM. This method is particularly appealing for its flexibility and ease of integration into daily life. It has been shown to improve fat loss, enhance metabolic health, and may even help in reducing the risk of type 2 diabetes

5:2 Method

The 5:2 approach differs significantly from daily fasting methods. On this plan, you eat typically on five days a weekend reduce your calorie intakes to about 500-600 calories on the other two days, which should be non-consecutive to avoid excessive fatigue or hunger. This method can be beneficial for weight loss and improving cardiovascular health without the daily restrictions of other fasting methods, making it a good option for those who cannot commit to everyday fasting.

Alternate Day Fasting (ADF)

Alternate-Day Fasting, as the name implies, alternates between a day of regular eating and a day of fasting or extremely restricted calorie intake (about 500 calories). This method is quite rigorous and can lead to significant weight loss and improvements in multiple biomarkers of disease. However, it may be challenging to sustain long-term, especially for those new to fasting.

Other Lesser-Known Methods

Eat-Stop-Eat

Eat-Stop-Eat is a diet plan created by dietitian Brad Pilon that calls for one or two 24-hour fasts every week. For instance, skipping dinner the day before and eating dinner the following day. This method can help reduce calorie intake substantially and is known to boost metabolism. However, complete 24-hour fasting can be mentally and physically challenging and might be more suitable for those who have experience with shorter fasts first.

Warrior Diet

The Warrior Diet is a severe type of daily fasting that entails consuming one substantial meal during a 4-hour eating window at night and little portions of raw fruits and vegetables during the day. The eating habits of ancient warriors, who ate sparingly during the day and lavishly at night, are the basis for this diet. It aims to improve the way the body processes nutrients and has a robust following, though it requires a significant lifestyle shift.

Spontaneous Meal Skipping

Unlike structured fasting methods, spontaneous meal skipping does not require a strict schedule. Instead, you skip meals when convenient. This could be breakfast one day, lunch another, and dinner another time. It's based on the premise that humans are naturally well-equipped to handle periods without food. This method is extremely flexible and can easily be adapted to any lifestyle without much preparation.

OMAD (One Meal a Day)

With OMAD, one must consume all of their daily calories at one meal, which equates to a 23-hour fast every day. This extreme form of fasting can lead to significant weight loss and health improvements but should be approached with caution. It's critical to make sure that this one meal is extremely nutrient-dense and includes every food category required to sustain health.

Choosing the right intermittent fasting method involves considering your health goals, lifestyle, and how your body responds to different fasting intervals. Starting with a less restricted approach, like the 16/8 plan, then working your way up to more rigid forms, like ADF or OMAD, if desired, is usually good. Before beginning any new diet plan, see a doctor, especially if you use medication or have any pre-existing health conditions. With the right plan and a clear understanding of how to implement it, One effective way to improve your health and wellbeing is through intermittent fasting.

Customizing Your Fasting Schedule

Adopting an intermittent fasting plan effectively requires a personalized approach tailored to individual lifestyles, daily routines, and personal health goals. Customizing your fasting schedule is essential for enhancing the benefits of intermittent fasting and ensuring it becomes a sustainable part of your lifestyle.

Assessing Lifestyle and Adapting Fasting

To begin, thoroughly assess your daily routine. Consider your wake-up time, work schedule, and periods of high activity. This initial assessment will help determine which fasting method might integrate seamlessly with your existing lifestyle. For instance, if your mornings are occupied with social and business breakfasts, a 16/8 fasting method with an eating window from 9 AM to 5 PM might interfere with these engagements. Alternatively, adjusting your eating window to start later in the day could accommodate both your professional and dietary needs without disruption.

Your social and family interactions also play a critical role in shaping your fasting schedule. Intermittent fasting should enhance rather than complicate your relationships. If family dinners are central to your daily life, align your eating window to ensure you can participate fully in these meals. This strategy helps maintain your social and familial bonds, ensuring that your dietary habits do not lead to social isolation or familial tension.

Moreover, your health status and specific nutritional needs must guide your fasting plan. If you have conditions such as diabetes or digestive issues, customize your fasting schedule to factor in these health considerations. Professional advice from healthcare providers can be invaluable in this customization, helping you safely and effectively integrate fasting into your lifestyle.

Balancing Fasting Windows with Life Demands

Flexibility is crucial in establishing a successful intermittent fasting regimen. While maintaining a consistent schedule can facilitate routine, too much rigidity can introduce unnecessary stress and lead to potential failure. Allowing yourself the flexibility to adapt your fasting windows based on fluctuating daily demands and energy requirements will likely enhance your experience and success with intermittent fasting.

Your workload and physical energy levels are also significant considerations. On days characterized by high physical demand or significant workload, adjust your fasting schedule to provide more substantial energy support. For example, positioning a larger meal post-workout can replenish energy stores and aid in muscle recovery, aligning your nutritional intake with your energy expenditures.

Exercise routines should be thoughtfully coordinated with your fasting schedule. If you prefer working out in the morning, plan your largest meal for after your exercise session, within your eating window, to maximize recovery and nutrient absorption. If evening workouts fit your schedule better, arrange your eating window to ensure you can eat soon after exercising, supporting optimal recovery and nutrient use.

It is also essentialmust pay attention to your body's signals. Modify the length of your fasting plan based on bodily responses to different fasting and feeding patterns. Symptoms like fatigue, irritability, or disrupted sleep are indicators that your current fasting plan may not be aligned with your physiological needs. Experiment with adjusting the duration of your fasts or the timing of your meals to find a balance that supports your health and well-being.

Starting with an initial fasting schedule and being open to making adjustments based on personal experience and body response will help you find the most suitable and sustainable method. This process of trial and adaptation is key to successfully integrating intermittent fasting into your life, ensuring that it not only improves your health but also complements your lifestyle. By personalizing your approach and allowing for adjustments, you can maintain a balanced and effective fasting regimen that supports your overall health goals.

What to Expect in the First Month

Embracing intermittent fasting involves more than just a change in diet; it's a comprehensive adjustment that affects your body, mind, and daily routines. The first month of intermittent fasting is particularly crucial as it is the period during which you and your physique learn to adapt to the new eating pattern. Understanding what to expect during this initial phase can help you manage the transition more effectively and set realistic expectations.

Physical and Emotional Adaptations

Adjustment Phase

Initially, your body will undergo a significant adjustment phase. Since it's accustomed to receiving food at regular intervals, the new fasting schedule might lead to feelings of hunger and a temporary decrease in energy as your body starts to recalibrate its usual feeding times. These sensations are normal and typically diminish as your body adapts to its new metabolic rhythm.

Energy Levels

During the first few days, you might feel unusually tired or weak. This occurs because your body, used to a constant supply of glucose from frequent meals, now needs to switch to burning fat for energy, a process known as ketosis. Once this transition is made, many people report a significant increase in energy levels and mental clarity toward the end of the first month.

Digestive Changes

You may experience changes in your digestive system, including constipation or diarrhea. These symptoms can result from changes in meal frequency and timing. Drinking plenty of water and increasing fiber intake can help manage these digestive changes.

Physical Performance

If you're physically active, you might notice a temporary decline in your performance specially during higher-intensity activities. This decrease is due to your body adapting to using fat as its primary energy source. Gradually, most individuals see a restoration or even an improvement in performance as their bodies become more efficient at fat-burning.

Emotional and Cognitive Responses

On the emotional front, you may find yourself feeling irritable or moody in the early days of fasting. These feelings are partly due to the hormonal changes associated with hunger. Moreover, psychological attachment to food routines can make it challenging to adopt new eating habits. However, as you progress, many report improvements in mood stability and a reduction in anxiety levels, attributed to better blood sugar management and reduced inflammation.

Managing Expectations

Setting Realistic Goals

Setting attainable objectives during the first month is crucial. Weight loss and health improvements occur gradually, and noticeable changes might take a bit longer than anticipated. Celebrate small victories like completing a fast without deviations or noticing you feel more alert.

Preparing for Social and Professional Settings

Prepare strategies for managing social and work environments where food is involved. Planning your eating windows around these events or choosing to partake moderately can help maintain your social relationships and prevent feelings of exclusion.

Flexible Adaptation

Be prepared to adjust your fasting plan based on your initial experiences. Flexibility in your approach allows you to tailor fasting methods as you learn more about how your body reacts. This adaptive strategy ensures that you are more likely to stick to intermittent fasting in the long run.

Support Systems

Having a support system can be incredibly beneficial. Engage with communities that focus on intermittent fasting, either online or in person. Sharing your experiences and hearing others' challenges and successes can provide encouragement and valuable insights.

Monitoring Health Metrics

Keep an eye on key health indicators such as weight, energy levels, sleep patterns, and digestive health. Tracking these can help you understand the impact of intermittent fasting on your body and guide necessary adjustments to your diet or fasting schedule.

The first month of intermittent fasting is about exploring and understanding your body's cues. It is a period marked by significant change, but with patience and careful management, you can set a foundation for sustainable health benefits. By the end of the first month, many of the initial challenges will begin to subside as you settle into your new routine, paving the way for more profound health improvements.

Fasting as a Lifestyle

Integrating intermittent fasting into your daily life as a sustainable practice is an enriching journey that enhances not only your physical health but also your overall quality of life. This integration requires understanding how to weave fasting into the fabric of your daily activities and commitments, ensuring it complements rather than complicates your existing routines.

Integrating Fasting Sustainably into Daily Life

Starting with intermittent fasting involves more than just skipping meals; it necessitates a thoughtful adjustment to when and how you eat. The key to sustainable fasting is finding a rhythm that works seamlessly with your personal and professional life. This may mean adapting your fasting periods to meet work schedules, social obligations, and family commitments. For instance, if your professional life involves frequent breakfast meetings, a fasting schedule that omits morning meals might not be suitable. Instead, a plan that places the fasting window later in the day or selects specific days for fasting could be more practical and sustainable.

The true essence of sustainability in fasting also lies in the ease with which it can be adapted over time. As your body adapts to intermittent fasting, you may find it easier to extend fasting periods or alter your eating window to enhance the benefits further. This flexibility allows you to maintain a fasting regimen that continues to challenge your body and promote health benefits without disrupting your daily life.

Long-Term Commitment and Flexibility

Embracing intermittent fasting as a long-term lifestyle choice requires a commitment not just to sticking with a schedule but also to remaining adaptable as your life changes. Life's circumstances can change dramatically—a new job, relocation, or changes in family dynamics—and your ability to maintain fasting during these times hinges on your flexibility. You may need to shift your fasting schedule or temporarily adjust your approach to fasting during particularly stressful or busy times.

Flexibility also means listening to your body and being willing to make changes based on what it needs. This could involve adjusting the length of your fasts, the size of your eating windows, or even the types of food you consume during your eating periods. For example, find you're frequently tired or hungry. It might be a sign to shorten your fasting window or reconsider what you're eating during non-fasting periods to ensure your diet remains balanced and nutritious.

A long-term commitment to fasting also implies embracing the practice as more than a diet—it's a shift in lifestyle that incorporates holistic changes to how you view food, health, and wellness. This perspective helps maintain motivation even when progress seems slow, as the benefits of fasting extend beyond weight loss to include improved metabolic health, better mental clarity, and a greater sense of well-being.

Including intermittent fasting in your lifestyle is a continuous practice that alters and adapts to your life's rhythms rather than a one-time alteration. It requires a balance of strictness to maintain discipline and the flexibility to adapt to life's realities. You can make sure that fasting stays a positive and fulfilling aspect of your life, one that can support not just your physical health but also your mental and emotional wellbeing, by developing a balanced attitude to it. Through thoughtful integration and committed flexibility, intermittent fasting can become not just a method for health improvement but a permanent fixture in your lifestyle landscape. –

Feedback and Adjustments

Integrating intermittent fasting into your lifestyle is an ongoing process that requires continual assessment and adaptation. Understanding how to monitor your progress and knowing when and how to make adjustments to your fasting plan is crucial for long-term success and maintaining the health benefits of intermittent fasting.

Monitoring progress during intermittent fasting isn't just about stepping on a scale; it involves a comprehensive approach to assessing both physical and emotional health improvements. Keeping a detailed journal can be immensely helpful in this regard. In this journal, record not only your weight but also other vital statistics such as body measurements and energy levels, along with more subjective metrics like mood and mental clarity. These notes will eventually give you a clear picture of how your body is reacting to the fasting schedule, enabling you to spot trends or outcomes that might not be obvious right away.

Maintaining a meal journal on a regular basis might be very beneficial to your intermittent fasting experience. This log will help you see not just when you eat but what you're eating, which is essential for understanding the nutritional balance of your diet. It can also help identify any dietary triggers that might be causing unexpected responses, such as bloating, lethargy, or irritability. With this information, adjustments can be made not only to the timing of your fasting but also to what you're consuming during your eating windows to optimize your health outcomes.

In addition to personal tracking, periodic medical check-ups can provide a more objective look at your health changes. Blood tests, for example, can track changes in cholesterol levels, liver function, inflammation markers, and more, offering a snapshot of your physiological changes under the surface. These tests can catch discrepancies that might not yet have manifested as physical symptoms, providing crucial data that can prompt timely adjustments to your fasting regimen.

Knowing when to adjust your fasting plan is just as important as knowing how. If you consistently need help with energy, for example, it might be a sign that your eating window needs to be bigger or properly timed. If you experience persistent hunger or irritability, it may indicate that the quality or quantity of food consumed during your eating periods is insufficient. Emotional signs such as feeling overwhelmed or stressed by your diet are also important indicators that your plan may require recalibration to fit your lifestyle and emotional needs better.

The adjustment process should be thoughtful and data-driven. Begin by identifying the specific issues you are encountering, then look at possible causes that align with these issues. Adjustments include shifting your fasting window, changing its duration, or modifying your dietary composition during eating windows. For instance, adding more protein and fibre might help alleviate feelings of hunger, while adjusting the timing of your last meal before starting your fast might help with energy levels the following day.

Flexibility is a cornerstone of successfully maintaining an intermittent fasting routine. This doesn't mean making frequent, random changes but rather making thoughtful adjustments based on a combination of subjective feedback from your personal experiences and objective data from health tracking and medical tests. This balanced approach ensures that your fasting regimen supports your health without detracting from your quality of life.

Embracing intermittent fasting as a lifestyle means being prepared to adapt not just to the initial changes but to the ongoing developments in your health and personal circumstances. With careful monitoring and the willingness to make thoughtful adjustments, intermittent fasting can continue to be a rewarding and health-promoting part of your life long after you've begun. By regularly assessing your progress and being willing to fine-tune your approach, you ensure that your fasting lifestyle evolves in harmony with your changing health needs and life situations.

CHAPTER 3

NUTRITION FUNDAMENTALS

Understanding nutrition is crucial, especially for women over 50, who face unique dietary needs as they age. This chapter explores the essential nutrients and minerals necessary for maintaining health during this stage of life, along with practical advice on making necessary adjustments to meet age-related dietary needs.

Nutritional Needs for Women Over 50

As women age, their bodies undergo significant changes that can affect nutritional requirements. Estrogen levels decline dramatically during menopause, impacting bone density and cardiovascular health. To counter these effects, certain nutrients become particularly important:

Calcium and Vitamin D: They're essential for keeping your bones healthy. Bone density tends to decrease in postmenopausal women, increasing the risk of osteoporosis. Calcium supports the structure of bones, while vitamin D enhances calcium absorption. About 1200 mg of calcium and 600 IU of vitamin D should be the daily goals for women over 50. Dairy products, dark green vegetables, and fortified meals are good sources of calcium. Sunlight exposure, fatty seafood, and supplements are good sources of vitamin D.

Iron: Iron needs to decrease after menopause since women are no longer menstruating. The recommended daily intake drops from 18 mg to 8 mg. However, iron remains a critical component for blood cell production and overall energy levels. Lean meats, shellfish, legumes, and spinach are all excellent providers of iron.

Vitamin B12: As we age, our bodies become less efficient at absorbing vitamin B12, which is essential for blood formation and brain functions. Older adults are often advised to get their vitamin B12 from fortified foods or supplements, as this form is more easily absorbed than the vitamin found in meat, fish, and dairy.

Fiber: Adequate fiber intake is crucial for maintaining digestive health, which can become sluggish with age. Fiber helps to prevent constipation and lowers cholesterol levels. It also plays a role in controlling blood sugar levels, which can help manage and prevent diabetes. Eating fruits, vegetables, whole grains, and legumes can help women over 50 reach their daily goal of at least 21 grams of fiber.

Antioxidants: As antioxidants, vitamins A, C, and E slow down the aging process by scavenging free radicals, which can harm cells and lead to long-term illnesses. Antioxidant-rich foods include dark chocolate, leafy greens, berries, almonds, and carrots.

Adjustments for Age-Related Dietary Needs

As women age, their metabolic rate slows down, which means they need fewer calories to maintain their weight. As a result, it becomes more crucial to select nutrient-dense foods that offer the necessary vitamins and minerals without being too caloric.

Protein: Maintaining muscle mass can be a challenge as women age, particularly after the age of 50. Adequate protein intake is essential for preserving muscle health. Good sources of high-quality protein include tofu, beans, lentils, and lean animal proteins.

Healthy Fats: Fats are essential for hormonal health, especially as estrogen levels decline. Pay attention to sources of heart-healthy fats that help lower inflammation and promote general heart health, such as nuts, seeds, avocados, and olive oil.

Reduced Sodium: High blood pressure is more common in postmenopausal women, and high sodium intake can exacerbate this condition. Lowering salt consumption to fewer than 2,300 mg daily—ideally, less than 1,500 mg for people with hypertension—can assist in controlling blood pressure.

Water: Older adults often experience a reduced sense of thirst, which can lead to dehydration. Drinking adequate fluids is crucial for maintaining kidney health and aiding in the digestion and absorption of nutrients.

By understanding and adjusting their diet to meet these specialized needs, women over 50 can significantly enhance their health and well-being. The secret is to concentrate on eating a diet high in nutrients that supplies vital vitamins and minerals to support bodily processes, control aging-related changes, and increase longevity. This proactive approach to nutrition can help mitigate the impacts of ageing and maintain a high quality of life during the golden years.

Eating Strategies during Feeding Windows

When intermittent fasting is practiced, meal windows are crucial for providing the body with all the nutrition it requires to perform at its best and endure the fasting intervals. It's not just about filling the stomach but rather making every calorie count towards your overall health, especially for women over 50 who have specific nutritional needs. This section delves into how to maximize nutrition intake during eating windows and offers practical meal planning ideas that align with a healthy fasting lifestyle.

Maximizing Nutrition Intake

The key to maximizing nutrition intake during eating windows involves focusing on nutrient density rather than calorie density. This entails selecting meals that are high in nutrients in comparison to their calorie count. Foods high in vitamins, minerals, antioxidants, and fiber that promote general health and aid in the management of age-related disorders include fruits, vegetables, lean meats, whole grains, and legumes.

A practical approach is to structure meals to include a variety of food groups, thus ensuring a balanced intake of nutrients. For instance, incorporating a lean protein source at each meal helps maintain muscle mass, which is crucial as muscle degradation accelerates with age. Pairing these proteins with fibrous vegetables and healthy fats can optimize fullness and nutrient absorption, aiding digestive health and enhancing metabolic efficiency.

To ensure adequate vitamin and mineral intake, especially those in which women over 50 are often deficient—such as calcium, iron, and vitamins D and B12—incorporating fortified foods or supplements as part of meal planning can be beneficial. For example, a breakfast of fortified whole-grain cereal with almond milk can provide a significant amount of daily calcium and vitamin D needs, while a lunch center around leafy greens and lean beef can cover iron and vitamin B12 requirements.

Focusing on hydration is equally important; older adults often experience diminished thirst perception, which can lead to dehydration. Including foods high in water content, such as cucumbers, tomatoes, and melons, and drinking ample fluids throughout the eating window can help maintain hydration and support kidney function and nutrient transportation.

Meal Planning Ideas

Planning meals can help avoid the temptation to break the fast with whatever is convenient, which often ends up being less nutritious. Instead, having a clear plan ensures that each meal is balanced and contributes to the overall nutritional goals. Here are some ideas for structuring meals to maximize nutritional intake:

Breakfast Ideas

A smoothie made with spinach, a scoop of protein powder, frozen berries, and flaxseed mixed with water or a dairy-free milk alternative. Omega-3 fatty acids, fiber, vitamins, antioxidants, and protein are all abundant in this dish.

Oatmeal cooked with almond milk and topped with walnuts and sliced apples. This recipe has an excellent balance of protein, soluble fiber, and heart-healthy fats that support cholesterol control and deliver long-lasting energy.

Lunch Ideas

Feta cheese, salad made of quinoa, cherry tomatoes, cucumbers, chickpeas, and olive oil and lemon juice. This provides a wonderful mix of plant-based protein, complex carbohydrates, healthy fats, and several vitamins and minerals.

A turkey and avocado wrap with whole grain tortillas served alongside a mixed greens salad with vinaigrette. This meal combines lean proteins, heart-healthy fats, and whole grains that contribute to cardiovascular health and satiety.

Dinner Ideas:

Grilled salmon with a side of steamed broccoli and sweet potato. Salmon is high in fatty acids omega-3, which are vital for heart and brain health, while sweet potatoes provide beta-carotene and complex carbohydrates

A stir-fry featuring a variety of vegetables and tofu or chicken breast, served over brown rice. This meal is high in protein, fibre, and essential nutrients while being balanced in macronutrients.

Planning meals and knowing exactly what to eat during the feeding window can significantly enhance the effectiveness of intermittent fasting. It ensures that every meal is nutrient-packed and contributes positively towards overall health, particularly for women over 50, who need to be mindful of their bone density, muscle mass, and metabolic health. By adopting these strategic eating practices, the fasting lifestyle can become not only sustainable but also enjoyable and highly beneficial to long-term health.

Hydration and Intermittent Fasting

Given that dehydration can have detrimental effects on metabolism and overall health, maintaining enough water is essential to the success of intermittent fasting.

Understanding the importance of maintaining adequate hydration and implementing effective strategies to enhance hydration is essential, especially for women over 50 who are practicing fasting.

Importance of Water and Other Fluids

Water is fundamental to life; it facilitates countless physiological processes, including digestion, nutrient absorption, and waste elimination. It also plays a vital role in maintaining blood volume and allowing proper circulation, which are crucial for optimal functioning of all bodily systems. During fasting periods, the body continues to require water to perform these basic functions, even in the absence of food intake.

For those practicing intermittent fasting, staying adequately hydrated is essential because it helps mitigate some of the initial side effects of fasting, such as headaches, lethargy, and irritability, which are often exacerbated by dehydration. Moreover, hydration helps maintain satiety levels, which can make fasting periods more manageable by reducing the perception of hunger.

Water isn't the only fluid that can contribute to hydration; other beverages, including herbal teas and bone broth, also count toward fluid intake. These alternatives not only help diversify the sources of hydration but can also provide other nutrients and compounds that aid digestive health, support metabolic processes, and enhance the body's ability to sustain longer periods of fasting.

Tips to Enhance Hydration

Enhancing hydration during intermittent fasting involves more than just drinking water; it requires a proactive and strategic approach to ensure fluid intake is optimal throughout both fasting and feeding periods. Here are some effective hydration strategies tailored for those engaged in intermittent fasting:

Start Your Day with Water: Begin your day with one or two glasses of water. Doing so can kickstart your hydration early, which is especially important if you send your eating window early in the evening. This routine promotes good hydration during the day and aids in replacing fluids lost over night.

Incorporate Hydrating Foods: During your eating windows, make an effort to include foods with high water content. Vegetables like cucumbers, lettuce, and zucchini, as well as fruits like oranges, strawberries, and watermelon, may make a substantial contribution to your daily water consumption. These meals are high in vitamins, minerals, and fiber, all of which are good for general health, in addition to being hydrated.

Use Herbal Teas: Herbal teas are excellent for staying hydrated during fasting windows because they are calorie-free and can be consumed hot or cold. Options like peppermint, chamomile, or hibiscus not only keep you hydrated but also offer relaxing and anti-inflammatory benefits, which can be particularly soothing during a fast.

Set Regular Drinking Reminders: It's easy to forget to drink water, especially when busy or distracted. Setting reminders to drink water can help maintain steady hydration throughout the day. Whether it's an alarm on your phone or a designated water-drinking schedule, consistent reminders can make a big difference in your hydration habits.

Monitor Hydration Levels: Pay attention to signs of dehydration, which include dark urine, dry skin, fatigue, and dizziness. These symptoms indicate that you need to increase your fluid intake. Consistently monitoring these signs will help you adjust your drinking habits before dehydration impacts your health.

Balance Electrolytes: During longer fasting periods, especially those over 24 hours, it's important to maintain electrolyte balance. Adding a pinch of salt to your water or consuming electrolyte supplements can help replenish sodium, potassium, and other essential electrolytes, ensuring that your cells function optimally and you remain hydrated.

Hydration is an essential component of a successful intermittent fasting regimen. By understanding the critical role of fluids and implementing strategies to ensure adequate daily intake, individuals practicing intermittent fasting can enhance their fasting experience, improve overall health outcomes, and maintain better hydration levels, making the fasting process both effective and sustainable.

Supplements to Consider

While intermittent fasting offers many health benefits, certain dietary restrictions can make it challenging to get all the necessary nutrients from food alone, especially for women over 50 who may have specific nutritional needs. Supplements can play a crucial role in filling these 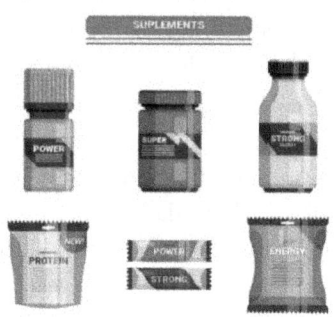 nutritional gaps. However, it is essential to approach supplementation with an understanding of what is necessary and what is not, as well as being aware of potential risks.

Necessary Vitamins and Minerals

During intermittent fasting, especially in diets limited during short eating windows or specific food groups, certain vitamins and minerals are critical to ensure comprehensive nutritional coverage:

Vitamin D: Vitamin D, often known as the "sunshine vitamin" because the body makes it in reaction to sunlight, is essential for healthy bones, a functioning immune system, and the decrease of inflammation. Given that many people live in climates with insufficient sunlight or have lifestyles that limit sun exposure, supplementation might be necessary. This is particularly important for older women, as Vitamin D absorption decreases with age.

Calcium: Essential for bone health, calcium is crucial, especially as women age and their risk for osteoporosis increases. While it can be consumed through dairy products and leafy greens, the bioavailability of calcium from these sources can vary, and supplementation may be needed to meet the daily requirements, especially if dairy is limited in the diet.

Magnesium: More than 300 biochemical processes in the body, including as those involving muscles and nerves, blood glucose management, and blood pressure regulation, are supported by this mineral. It is also essential for the metabolism of Vitamin D. Magnesium can be found in nuts, grains, beans, and dark, leafy vegetables, but supplementation might be necessary if these foods are underrepresented in the diet.

Iron: Iron is critical to prevent anaemia, particularly for women who have not yet reached menopause. Although their requirements are lower, post-menopausal women still need to maintain adequate iron levels. If more than dietary intake is required, especially in vegetarian or vegan diets, iron supplements might be considered.

Omega-3 Fatty Acids: These are essential for cardiovascular health, brain function, and inflammation control. The body does not typically produce omega-3s, which must be obtained from fatty fish, flaxseed, or supplements like fish oil or algae-based omega-3s. This can be particularly important for individuals who do not consume fish.

B Vitamins: Particularly vitamin B12, which is crucial for blood formation and brain health. B12 is primarily found in animal products, and those on a plant-based diet will likely need to take supplements to meet their needs.

Recommendations and Cautions

While supplements can significantly support a healthy diet, especially under the constraints of intermittent fasting, they should be used judiciously:

Consult with a Healthcare Provider: Speak with a healthcare provider before beginning any supplement program, especially if you use other drugs or have pre-existing health concerns. This phase guarantees that any supplements are required, considering your unique health profile and nutritional intake, and won't conflict with any prescriptions or medical problems.

Quality and Dosage: Opt for high-quality brands that have been third-party tested for purity and accuracy of dosage. This is crucial because dietary supplements are regulated differently than pharmaceuticals in many countries, which can lead to discrepancies between what the label claims and what the supplement actually contains.

Be Wary of Over-supplementation: Not everything that is more is necessarily better. When consumed in excess, fat-soluble vitamins like A, D, E, and K can build up in the body and become poisonous. High concentrations of some elements, such as zinc and iron, can also cause imbalances and health problems by interfering with the absorption of other minerals and each other.

Periodic Re-evaluation: Nutritional needs can change over time due to age, health status, and diet changes. Regularly re-evaluating your supplement needs can help adjust your intake accordingly and prevent both deficiencies and excesses.

Incorporating the right supplements into your diet while practicing intermittent fasting can help maintain optimal health, support the effectiveness of your fasting regimen, and prevent nutritional deficiencies, especially in women over 50 who may be at increased risk for specific nutritional gaps. With careful consideration and professional guidance, supplements can be a valuable addition to an intermittent fasting lifestyle.

Avoiding Nutritional Pitfalls

Integrating intermittent fasting into your lifestyle can bring substantial health benefits, particularly for women over 50 who are managing changes in metabolism and hormone levels. However, like any dietary regimen, there are common pitfalls that can undermine its effectiveness and even lead to health issues if not properly managed. Understanding these pitfalls and learning how to avoid them is crucial to maintaining optimal health and achieving the desired benefits of intermittent fasting.

Common Dietary Mistakes

Those who are new to intermittent fasting frequently make the grave error of focusing on the quality of their meals during eating periods. There's a tendency to focus solely on calorie intake rather than the nutritional content of the food being eaten. This may result in eating meals that are high in calories but poor in nutrients—a.k.a. "empty calories." Such foods include processed snacks, sugary beverages, and high-fat fast foods, which can contribute to nutrient deficiencies, weight gain, and metabolic issues.

Another frequent error is overeating during feeding periods. Some people compensate for the hours they've fasted by consuming an excessive amount of food when they do eat, mistakenly thinking this balances out the fasting period. This can not only disrupt metabolic health but also lead to a slower metabolism as the body struggles to process a large amount of food at once.

Additionally, many need to hydrate adequately. During fasting periods, there's no food intake to provide some of the water your body needs. If this isn't compensated for by increasing fluid intake during eating windows, it can lead to dehydration. Dehydration not only impairs physical functions but also reduces the effectiveness of the fasting process itself by worsening symptoms like headaches and fatigue, which can discourage adherence to the fasting regimen.

Skipping a variety of food groups is another common issue. Some might avoid carbohydrates or fats entirely, mistakenly believing this will enhance the benefits of fasting. However, this can lead to deficiencies in vital nutrients and the beneficial effects of these macronutrients, such as energy provision and cellular function, respectively.

How to Overcome Them

It's critical to concentrate on a balanced diet that incorporates a range of food categories in order to avoid making these dietary errors. Ensure that each meal is composed of vegetables, fruits, whole grains, lean proteins, and healthy fats. This not only provides a range of essential nutrients but also helps maintain muscle mass and support metabolic health, which is particularly crucial for older women.

Another key strategy is practicing portion control. Rather than eating large meals infrequently, aim to consume smaller, more balanced meals throughout the eating window. This can help prevent the temptation to overeat and support better metabolic regulation. It's helpful to use smaller plates, check serving sizes on food labels, and be mindful of the body's hunger and fullness signals.

Make an effort to stay hydrated by drinking fluids regularly throughout the day, not just while you're eating. Including high-water foods like celery, cucumbers, and watermelon can also help you stay hydrated. Additionally, herbal teas and broths can be included during fasting periods as they provide hydration without breaking the fast.

Ensure to include all macronutrients in your diet. Proteins are necessary for muscle growth and repair, lipids are necessary for hormonal balance and vitamin absorption, and carbohydrates are necessary for energy. Choosing complex carbohydrates like whole grains, high-quality proteins like fish and legumes, and healthy fats from avocados and nuts ensures a rich nutrient intake and helps avoid deficiencies.

By avoiding these common dietary mistakes and implementing thoughtful, balanced eating strategies, women over 50 can enhance the effectiveness of intermittent fasting. By supporting their unique nutritional demands and fostering improved health outcomes, this strategy allows patients to reap the rewards of intermittent fasting while continuing to lead fulfilling lives.

CHAPTER 4

EXERCISE INTEGRATION

Integrating exercise into an intermittent fasting regimen enhances the benefits of both practices, promoting a synergistic effect that can significantly improve overall health, particularly for women over 50. Understanding how exercise complements intermittent fasting and identifying the best times for workouts is crucial for maximizing these health benefits.

Benefits of Exercise While Fasting

Exercise during fasting periods can amplify the physiological effects of fasting itself. The key benefit of intermittent fasting lies in the transition from glucose metabolism to fat breakdown, or ketosis, as the predominant energy source. When exercise is introduced, especially aerobic activities like walking, running, or cycling, the body accelerates the use of fat as an energy source, enhancing fat loss.

Additionally, fasting leads to increased production of the hormone norepinephrine, which aids the body inbreak down fat to be used as fuel. Exercise increases this effect by speeding up the metabolism, which not only helps during the workout but also continues the enhanced fat burning for hours afterwards. This is particularly beneficial for women over 50, who often experience a slowdown in metabolism as part of the ageing process.

Exercise can also assist in reducing some of the negative effects of fasting, such as blood sugar swings. By helping regulate glucose and improving insulin sensitivity, exercise makes fasting periods more manageable andhas the potential to lower type 2 diabetes risk .

It also boosts endorphins, the body's natural mood elevators, which can be especially useful to combat the mood swings and irritability that can sometimes accompany fasting.

How Exercise Complements Intermittent Fasting

Integrating exercise into a fasting schedule helps optimize the body's adaptation to burn fat more efficiently. During fasting, glycogen stores in the liver are depleted, and the body starts to mobilize fat as an energy source. When exercise is added to the mix, this process is accelerated, and the increase in metabolic rate can lead to more effective weight management and body composition changes. Furthermore, the combination of fasting and exercise has been shown to increase mitochondrial density, which improves the body's ability to produce energy, enhancing overall physical stamina and resilience.

The body uses autophagy, which is enhanced by exercise, to eliminate damaged cells and replace them with new ones. This process is naturally increased during fasting, but exercising while fasting can further boost this beneficial cellular mechanism. Autophagy is crucial for preventing diseases such as Alzheimer's and cancer, which becomes increasingly important with advancing age.

Best Times for Workouts

Choosing the best time to exercise during intermittent fasting can depend largely on personal preference and individual schedules, but some general guidelines can help optimize the effects:

Morning Workouts: Exercising in the morning, particularly before the first meal, can maximize fat burning because energy derived from the last meal has been used up, forcing the body to use its fat stores. This is ideal for those aiming for weight loss and improved metabolic flexibility.

Mid-day or Evening Workouts: If morning workouts are not feasible, exercising right before breaking a fast can also be effective. For instance, if your eating window is from 12 p.m. to 8 p.m., scheduling a workout just before noon can allow you to replenish your body immediately after exercising, optimizing recovery and muscle synthesis with nutrient-rich foods.

Consistency Is Key: More important than the specific time of day is the consistency of the exercise routine. Regular physical activity, regardless of the time, contributes significantly to the health benefits associated with intermittent fasting.

Incorporating regular exercise into an intermittent fasting regimen not only enhances the physical benefits but also helps maintain mental and emotional balance, which is particularly valuable for women over 50 as they navigate significant life transitions. By understanding how and when to integrate exercise into a fasting schedule, it is possible to significantly enhance the efficacy of both practices, promoting better health outcomes and a more active and fulfilling lifestyle.

Cardiovascular Exercises

Exercise that uses your heart and breathing muscles in a repeated, rhythmic manner while working vast muscle groups is referred to as cardiovascular exercise, or cardio. It is foundational to improving heart health, increasing lung capacity, and effectively burning calories and fat. For those integrating cardio with intermittent fasting, the timing, intensity, and type of cardio can be pivotal in maximizing the benefits of both practices.

Recommended Routines

Walking or Jogging

- **Routine**: Begin with brisk walking, gradually transitioning to jogging as your fitness improves. Aim for 30 to 45 minutes per session, three to five times a week.
- **Progression**: Start with a comfortable pace where you can maintain a conversation. Increase your speed or incline gradually over weeks.

Cycling:

- **Routine**: Start with steady-state cycling for 20-30 minutes at a moderate pace. Indoor or outdoor cycling both provide excellent cardiovascular workouts.
- **Progression**: Introduce intervals by cycling hard for 1-2 minutes, followed by 2-3 minutes of easy cycling. Increase the length and intensity of the hard intervals over time.

Swimming:

- **Routine:** Begin with 20 minutes of continuous swimming using any stroke that maintains a moderate pace. Aim to swim three times a week.
- **Progression**: Increase the duration by 5 minutes each week until you can swim for 40-45 minutes. Start incorporating faster laps or more challenging strokes to increase intensity.

Aerobics Classes

- **Routine**: Join a class that fits your fitness level. Standard aerobics or dance classes that keep you moving continuously are great for beginners.

- **Progression:** As you gain fitness, move into more intense classes such as step aerobics, Zumba, or kickboxing. Increase the number of classes you attend per week.

Rowing

- **Routine:** Start with a 15-minute session at a moderate pace. Rowing is an excellent full-body workout that is also easy on the joints.
- **Progression:** Increase duration first, then add intervals of intense rowing for 1-2 minutes, followed by moderate rowing for 2-3 minutes.

How to Start and Progress

Getting Started

1. **Assess Fitness Level:** Before beginning any cardio routine, assess your current fitness level. This assessment will help you choose the right starting intensity and avoid overexertion, which can lead to injuries or demotivation.
2. **Choose the Right Activity:** Pick an activity you enjoy. Enjoyment is a significant factor in long-term exercise adherence. Whether it's running, cycling, swimming, or aerobics, your choice should fit your lifestyle and physical condition.
3. **Equip Appropriately:** Invest in the right gear. Good running shoes, a comfortable bicycle, swim goggles, or specific class equipment can make a difference in your performance and enjoyment.
4. **Plan Your Schedule:** If you are intermittent fasting, align your cardio workouts with your eating windows. Many find that cardio feels best after the first meal of the day when energy levels are replenished.

Progression Tips:

1. **Incremental Increases**: The key to progression without injury or burnout is a gradual increase. Whether it's adding 5 minutes to your cardio session each week or increasing the intensity of your intervals, small increments ensure steady improvement.
2. **Mix It Up**: To avoid plateaus, vary your routine. Include different types of cardio exercises in your weekly schedule. This increases overall fitness and challenges various muscle groups, all while keeping the routine engaging.
3. **Listen to Your Body**: It's important to pay attention to your body's cues, particularly during fasting.
4. If you feel dizzy, overly tired, or unwell, adjust your intensity or consider consuming a balanced meal or snack before your workout.
5. **Set Realistic Goals**: Setting achievable goals can provide motivation and a sense of accomplishment. Whether it's you're improving time, distance, or simply the frequency of your workouts, having clear goals can guide your progression.

Integrating cardiovascular exercises into your intermittent fasting schedule can amplify your health benefits, from better metabolic rates to improved cardiovascular health and more effective weight management. By starting appropriately, progressing wisely, and staying consistent, you can build a cardiovascular routine that not only fits your lifestyle but also enhances your fasting experience.

Strength Training

Strength training is a critical component of an overall fitness regimen, especially for individuals over 50. As we age, we naturally lose muscle mass and strength, a condition known as sarcopenia. Strength training can counteract this decline, improving muscle mass, strengthening bones, and enhancing overall quality of life. Integrating strength training into your routine requires understanding how to build muscle safely at this stage of life.

Building Muscle at Over 50

Building muscle after 50 is not only possible but also essential for maintaining functional independence and metabolic health. Age-related losses in muscle mass are a natural occurrence, however resistance exercise can greatly halt or even reverse this tendency.

Progressive Overload

Using the idea of progressive overload—which calls for progressively increasing the weight utilized or the intensity of exercises—is essential to building muscle. Starting with lighter weights or less intense sessions is important; But as you get stronger, you have to gradually test your muscles by adding more weight or resistance to encourage muscular growth.

High-Quality Protein Intake

Muscle repair and growth necessitate adequate protein consumption. Older adults, in particular, may need higher amounts of dietary protein than younger individuals to maintain and build muscle mass effectively. Incorporating sources of high-qualityproteins like fish and lean meatseggs, dairy products, and legumes in your diet is vital, especially post-workout when muscle repair is optimal.

Compound Movements

Exercises that work multiple muscle groups simultaneously are particularly effective for building muscle. These include squats, deadlifts, bench presses, and rows. These movements engage several joints and muscles, promoting hormonal responses conducive to muscle growth and making your workouts more time-efficient.

Consistency and Recovery

Consistency in your workout schedule is crucial for muscle building. Make an effort to perform two or three strength training sessions per week, and be sure to provide adequate time for recovery in between. Muscles need time to repair and grow stronger, so incorporating rest days is essential.

Safe Practices

Safety is paramount when it comes to strength training, especially for those over 50, as they are at a higher risk of injuries.

Proper Warm-up

It is crucial to start each session with a proper warm-up. Warm-up activities should involve light aerobic movement to increase heart rate and blood flow to muscles, followed by dynamic stretches to prepare the joints and muscles for the workout. This routine reduces the risk of injuries and can improve performance.

Technique over Weight

Focusing on the correct form is more important than the amount of weight lifted. Poor form can quickly lead to injuries, particularly to the back, shoulders, and knees. Consider working with a fitness professional initially to ensure your technique is correct. Once proper form is mastered, you can gradually increase the weight while maintaining that form.

Use Full Range of Motion

Performing movements through their full range of motion is essential unless restricted by pain. This practice ensures that all parts of the muscle are engaged and maximizes growth and flexibility.

Listen to Your Body

It's important to pay heed to your body's cues. Pain that goes beyond the normal stiffness in your muscles might be a sign that you are pushing too hard or that your technique is incorrect. Reducing the weight or intensity and focusing on recovery practices, such as stretching, hydration, and consulting healthcare providers, can help manage and prevent serious injuries.

Stay Hydrated and Rest

Hydration aids in protein synthesis and helps prevent injuries by keeping the tissues flexible and resilient. Proper sleep and rest are equally important as they are critical times when muscle repair and growth occur.

Incorporating strength training into an intermittent fasting and exercise regimen for those over 50 not only supports muscle maintenance and growth but also contributes significantly to metabolic health, bone density, and independence. By following these guidelines for safe practices and effective muscle-building strategies, older adults can enjoy the myriad benefits that strength training has to offer, enhancing both physical health and overall well-being.

Flexibility and Balance

As the body ages, maintaining flexibility and balance becomes increasingly crucial. These elements are fundamental not only for general mobility and daily activities but also for preventing falls, which are a common and serious concern for individuals over 50. Enhancing flexibility and balance through targeted exercises can significantly improve quality of life and independence.

Importance for Aging Bodies

The range of mobility that your joints can achieve is referred to as flexibility. Age-related alterations in tendons and muscles can weaken this quality, increasing the risk of injury, stiffness, and reduced mobility. Improving flexibility helps to alleviate muscle tension and can enhance posture, which is often compromised in older adults due to lifestyle factors and natural physiological changes.

Balance is equally critical as it declines with age, largely due to reduced muscle strength, poorer joint function, and other age-related neurological changes. Good balance is essential not only for everyday activities such as walking and climbing stairs but also as a preventive measure against falls, which can lead to significant disability.

Thus, especially as one ages, including activities that enhance balance and flexibility can be quite important for preserving independence and avoiding accidents. These exercises help keep the muscles elastic and the joints lubricated, ensuring smoother movements and less prone to strain.

Exercises to Include

Yoga

Yoga is an excellent activity for enhancing both flexibility and balance. It combines physical postures with breath control and meditation, which can also help reduce stress, another factor that can affect physical stability. Poses such as Tree Pose, Warrior III, and Chair Pose specifically strengthen the lower body and core, critical areas for balance maintenance.

Pilates

The core—the pelvis, abdomen, hips, and back—is the center of attention in Pilates because these body parts are essential for stability and balance. Exercises like the single leg stretch, Pilates roll-up, and leg circles not only improve core strength but also enhance flexibility through dynamic movements and stretching.

Tai Chi

This martial art is gentle and involves slow, controlled movements coupled with deep breathing. Numerous studies have demonstrated that Tai Chi is very useful for enhancing balance and lowers the incidence of falls in older persons. The fluid motions help maintain muscle softness and joint flexibility.

Stretching Routines:

Incorporating a daily stretching routine can significantly improve joint flexibility. Static stretches, where you hold a single position for a period, are particularly beneficial after exercising. Dynamic stretches are a great way to warm up before an exercise session since they include moving different portions of your body while progressively increasing your reach, speed, or both.

Balance Exercises:

Simple balances exercises can be performed anywhere and often require no special equipment. Practices such as standing on one foot, walking heel to toe, and balance walks (tightrope walks) are effective. As balance improves, these exercises can be made more challenging by closing the eyes or standing on a cushion.

Strength Training with a Focus on Lower Body:

Exercises that strengthen the legs and improve joint function can also enhance balance. Squats, lunges, and step-ups are beneficial. Using free weights or resistance bands while performing these exercises can further improve muscle strength and joint stability.

For aging bodies, it is important to incorporate these workouts into a regular fitness regimen. The combination of improved flexibility through stretching and yoga, enhanced core strength and stability through Pilates and strength training, and better neuromuscular coordination through Tai Chi provides a comprehensive approach to maintaining balance and flexibility. This holistic strategy not only promotes better mobility and independence but also contributes to overall health and well-being, allowing individuals over 50 to lead active, fulfilling lives free from the constraints often imposed by age-related physical changes.

Cycling (Stationary or Outdoor)

Cycling, whether stationary or outdoor, is a highly effective form of exercise that offers extensive benefits for individuals of all ages, including women over 50.

It combines cardiovascular fitness with leg strength development and can be a joyful, low-impact alternative to higher-stress exercises.

How to Perform

Outdoor Cycling

1. Choose the Right Bike:
   Ensure the bike fits your body to avoid discomfort. The seat

height should be adjusted so your legs are almost fully extended at the bottom of your pedal strokes.
2. Safety Gear: Wear appropriate safety gear including a helmet, and if necessary, knee and elbow pads.
3. Starting Out: Begin on flat, smooth surfaces. As confidence and stamina increase, you can explore varied terrain and longer distances.
4. Posture: Keep your shoulders loose, elbows slightly bent, and your head forward in a comfortable position.

5. Stationary Cycling

1. Adjusting the Bike: Adjust the saddle and handlebar height so that when you're sitting on the bike, your leg has a slight bend when the pedal is at its lowest point.
2. Getting Started: Begin with a gentle warm-up at a low resistance for 5-10 minutes.
3. Workout Session: Gradually increase the resistance to a level that is challenging yet manageable. Alternate between higher and lower intensities for interval training, or maintain a steady pace for endurance training.
4. Cool Down: End each session with a 5-minute cool-down at a reduced intensity and lower resistance.

Benefits

- Cardiovascular Health: By raising heart rate and fostering healthy blood flow, regular cycling lowers the risk of cardiovascular illnesses and improves heart health.
- Leg Strength and Endurance: It strengthens and increases the endurance of the quadriceps, hamstrings, calves, and glutes.
- Low Impact: Especially beneficial for women over 50 as it reduces stress on the knees, hips, and ankles compared to running.
- Weight Management: Helps burn calories and fat, which is beneficial in managing weight and metabolic health.

- Mental Health: Both outdoor and stationary cycling can decrease stress levels and improve mental health due to the release of endorphins, particularly with outdoor cycling, which also offers scenic stimulation and fresh air.

Equipment Needed

- Outdoor Cycling:
- A bicycle adjusted to fit
- Helmet and safety gear
- Optional: Cycling computer to track distance and speed

Stationary Cycling:

- A stationary exercise bike
- No additional equipment needed, although a heart rate monitor can be useful for tracking intensity

Cycling is adaptable and enjoyable, making it an ideal exercise for intermittent fasting lifestyles. It not only complements the fasting by enhancing calorie burn and promoting fat utilization but also supports overall well-being, making it a holistic exercise choice for women over 50.

Brisk Walking

Brisk walking is a simple, yet powerful, low-impact exercise suitable for people of all ages, including women over 50.

It involves walking at a faster pace than casual strolling, and it is an excellent way to improve cardiovascular health, enhance mood, and increase physical stamina without the stress on joints associated with higher-impact exercises.

How to Perform

1. Warm-Up: Begin with a 5-minute slow walk to gently raise your heart rate and loosen up your muscles.
2. Setting the Pace: Step up your pace until you can maintain a conversation while walking at a pace that causes your heart rate to rise.
3. This is typically about 3 to 4 miles per hour depending on fitness levels.
4. Posture: Look forward with your head held high, not down at the floor. Instead of standing rigidly straight, your back, shoulders, and neck should be relaxed. With a small bend in your elbows, freely swing your arms. It's acceptable to slightly pump your arms.
5. Stride: Use a natural stride length but focus on the roll through from heel to toe to push off for the next step.
6. Duration: Try to walk quickly for at least thirty minutes. If 30 minutes seems long at first, begin with 10- to 15-minute sessions and work your way up to a longer one.
7. Cool Down: Slow your pace down for the last 5 minutes to cool down, followed by some gentle stretching to enhance flexibility and prevent muscle stiffness.

Benefits

1. Improves Cardiovascular Health: Frequent brisk walking lowers the risk of cardiovascular disorders such high blood pressure, heart attacks, and strokes by strengthening the heart, improving blood circulation, and raising heart rate.
2. Promotes Better Oxygen Distribution Throughout the Body: Increased breathing rates brought on by fast walking can help the lungs function more efficiently and enhance pulmonary health.

3. Strengthens Muscles: Walking regularly strengthens the leg and abdominal muscles, and when done properly, arm motion can also help tone the arms, shoulders, and upper back.
4. Weight Management: Helps burn calories steadily, which can be particularly beneficial for weight management—a key concern for many women over 50.
5. Boosts Mental Health: It can also reduce anxiety, depression, and stress levels due to the increased release of endorphins.
6. Increases Bone Density: Frequent walking decreases the incidence of osteoporosis and enhances bone density by stressing the bones.
7. **Equipment Needed**
   - Proper Footwear: Wear comfortable, supportive walking shoes that provide good cushioning for your feet.
   - Clothing: Appropriate clothing for the weather—light layers for cold weather, and breathable fabrics for hot weather to maintain comfort throughout your walk.
   - Optional: While not required, a smartphone app or fitness tracker can be useful for tracking distance and pace.

Brisk walking is an accessible form of exercise that integrates seamlessly into any lifestyle. For women over 50, especially those practicing intermittent fasting, it provides a balanced approach to maintaining health without overstraining the body. It's an excellent way to clear the mind, improve health metrics, and enhance overall well-being with minimal investment and preparation.

Swimming

Swimming is a highly beneficial full-body exercise that is especially advantageous for women over 50. Because water is buoyant, it lessens the impact of movement and offers a full exercise that is easy on the joints. Swimming works the back, arms, legs, and core, among other muscle groups in the body, making it a great exercise for flexibility, cardiovascular health, and general fitness.

How to Perform

1. Warm-Up: Begin with light stretching on the poolside to loosen up your joints and muscles. Start your session with 2-3 laps of easy swimming to raise your body temperature and prepare your muscles for a more intense workout.
2. Technique Focus: Choose a stroke that feels comfortable for you; the freestyle (front crawl) is a common choice due to its natural motion and effectiveness. Ensure your technique is correct to avoid injuries:
3. Freestyle: Keep your body flat and horizontal. Turn your head to breathe - one goggle in the water, one out. Keep your arms extended and your kicks gentle and consistent.
4. Duration and Intensity: Initially, aim for swimming for at least 20-30 minutes per session. Maintain a pace that allows you to breathe easily but is fast enough to increase your heart rate. Over time, increase both the duration and intensity of your workouts as your endurance improves.
5. Cool Down: End your swimming session with slower, more relaxed laps to bring your heart rate down gradually. Follow

up with some stretching exercises outside the pool to help your muscles recover and reduce stiffness.

Benefits

1. Cardiovascular Fitness: Swimming increases the heart rate and promotes heart and lung health, enhancing cardiovascular fitness without straining the heart.
2. Muscle Tone and Strength: It provides a good muscle workout as water resistance is substantially higher than air resistance, engaging multiple muscle groups and building strength evenly.
3. Flexibility: The broad range of motion involved in swimming not only helps improve flexibility but also enhances muscular balance and posture.
4. Low Impact on Joints: Your body's weight is supported by the buoyancy of water, which eases joint strain.
5. This makes swimming ideal for those with arthritis or those recovering from injury.
6. Weight Management: As a high-calorie-burning exercise, swimming is excellent for weight management and can be particularly beneficial when combined with a diet like intermittent fasting.
7. Mental Health Benefits: Similar to other forms of exercise, swimming can decrease stress levels, improve mood, and decrease anxiety and depression symptoms through the release of endorphins.

Equipment Needed

- Swimsuit: Wear a comfortable, well-fitting swimsuit to ensure ease of movement.
- Goggles: Protects your eyes from chlorine in the pool and improves underwater visibility.

- Swimming Cap: Helps to keep your hair out of your face and reduce drag.
- Ear Plugs: Optional, to prevent water from entering the ear canal, especially if prone to ear infections.
- Towels and Swim Bag: Essential for drying off and carrying your swimming gear.

Swimming is a fantastic exercise for women over 50 looking to improve their health without heavy impact on their bodies. It is a holistic method to staying healthy during and after the middle years since it promotes not just physical health but also makes a substantial contribution to psychological well-being.

Pilates

Pilates is an exercise style that places a focus on the body's balanced growth via awareness, flexibility, and core strength to facilitate fluid, effective movement. It is particularly well-suited to women over 50 as it is low impact, focuses on muscular endurance, and does not strain the joints. Pilates can be an excellent choice for maintaining posture, muscle tone, and balance, which are crucial as the body ages.

How to Perform

1. Getting Started: Begin with a basic warm-up to loosen your muscles. This can include simple stretches and gentle movements that mimic the exercises you will perform.

2. Core Focus: Pilates exercises are centered around the core, which includes the abdominals, lower back, and hips. Ensure that you engage your core throughout each exercise to stabilize your midsection and protect your lower back.
3. Breathing: Proper breathing is essential in Pilates. Inhale deeply through the nose to prepare for movement, and exhale through the mouth as you perform the exertion part of the exercise. This helps activate the core muscles and maintain focus.
4. Pilates Movements: Some foundational Pilates exercises include:
5. The Hundred: A breathing exercise that also targets the abdominal muscles.
6. The Roll-Up: A slow, precise move that stretches the spine and increases flexibility.
7. Leg Circles: Which enhance hip joint flexibility and strengthen the leg muscles.
8. Plank: Which is excellent for building endurance in both the abdominal and back muscles.
9. Duration: Typically, a Pilates session lasts for about 45 to 60 minutes. You can start with shorter sessions to build your stamina.
10. Cool Down: Conclude your session with a series of stretches to relax and lengthen the muscles worked during the session.

Benefits

1. Core Strength: Pilates strengthens the muscles of the torso, improving posture, alleviating lower back pain, and enhancing overall fitness.
2. Increased Flexibility and Balance: Regular practice increases the range of motion for the joints and improves stability and balance, which is particularly beneficial in preventing falls as you age.

3. Low Impact: Suitable for those with joint issues or overall stiffness, as it improves muscle tone and fitness without stressing the joints.
4. Mind-Body Connection: Pilates encourages mindfulness through controlled movements and breathwork, enhancing mental clarity and emotional calm.
5. Improved Body Awareness: Heightened awareness of body positioning and movement helps correct imbalances and prevent injury.

Equipment Needed

- Pilates Mat: Thicker than a standard yoga mat to cushion the body.
- Pilates Ball: Helps in developing balance and enhancing core stability.
- Resistance Bands: Used to add resistance to Pilates exercises, increasing their difficulty and effectiveness.
- Pilates Ring: Optional, for adding intensity to various exercises, particularly for leg and arm workouts.

Pilates provides a superb blend of physical and mental conditioning that promotes both mental and physical wellbeing. For women over 50, it provides the tools to maintain vigor, posture, and health, and to navigate the physical changes that come with aging gracefully and actively.

Strength Training with Dumbbells

Strength training with dumbbells is an essential exercise regimen for women over 50, focusing on building muscle mass and strengthening bones. This form of exercise is crucial for combating age-related muscle loss and osteoporosis, a common concern for post-menopausal women. Dumbbell exercises are versatile, can be adjusted for any skill level, and can target every major muscle group in the body.

How to Perform

1. Warm-Up: To prepare the muscles and joints for lifting weights, begin with a general warm-up that consists of five to ten minutes of light aerobic exercise, such as walking or jogging in place. Next, perform dynamic stretches.
2. Choosing Weights: Choose dumbbells that are heavy enough to make the final 2-3 repetitions of an exercise challenging but still enabling you to perform 12–15 reps with proper technique. To learn the technique, start with smaller weights and work your way up to a larger weight as your strength increases.
1. **Execution**

Bicep Curls: Place your feet shoulder-width apart and keep your arms at your sides while grasping dumbbells with your hands facing front. Elbows should be kept close to the body when curling the weights. Return the weights to their initial positions slowly.

Triceps Extensions: Arms straight, both hands raised over the head to hold a dumbbell. Bend your elbows to bring it down behind your head, then lift it back up to the beginning.

Shoulder Press: Holding dumbbells at shoulder height with your hands facing ahead, stand or sit with your back straight. Press the weights above your head until your arms are straight. Go back to where you were before.

Squats: With dumbbells at your shoulders or at your sides, hold them. Maintain a straight back and place your knees over your toes while bending your knees and lowering your torso as if you were sitting back in a chair with your feet hip-width apart. Raise yourself back to a standing position.

Cool Down: Stretching gently for five to ten minutes helps to enhance flexibility and assist relax the muscles at the end of each exercise.

Benefits

- Enhances Muscle Mass: Regular strength training increases muscle fiber size, enhancing overall muscle mass, which naturally declines with age.
- Strengthens Bones: Dumbbell workouts assist to lower the risk of osteoporosis and build bone density since they include weight bearing.
- Improves Joint Health: Strength exercise can lessen the symptoms of arthritis and preserve joint flexibility.
- Boosts Metabolic Rate: Gaining muscle mass increases metabolic rate considerably, which helps control weight and increases energy.
- Enhances Functional Independence: Building strength helps maintain balance and coordination, crucial for daily activities and reducing the risk of falls.

Equipment Needed

- Dumbbells: A set of dumbbells in various weights. Adjustable dumbbells are a space-saving option that allows for varied resistance.
- Exercise Mat: Provides cushioning and support for floor exercises.
- Weight Bench (optional): Allows for a greater range of motion and support for exercises like bench press and tricep extensions.

Strength training with dumbbells offers comprehensive benefits that are particularly valuable for women over 50, supporting physical health, functional ability, and independence. Integrating this practice into your fitness regimen can help maintain and enhance quality of life and overall well-being.

Resistance Band Exercises

Resistance band exercises provide a versatile strength-training option that is particularly suitable for women over 50. These exercises use elastic bands that offer varying levels of resistance and are excellent for enhancing strength without the need for heavy weights, which can be cumbersome and intimidating. Resistance bands are gentle on the joints and can be used to target nearly every major muscle group, improving flexibility, strength, and range of motion.

How to Perform

Warm-Up: Start by engaging in aerobic exercises, such as walking or light running, for five to ten minutes to raise your heart rate and warm up your muscles. Dynamic stretches should be performed after to prime your body for workout.

- Choosing the Right Band: Resistance bands come in various thicknesses and strengths, typically indicated by color. Start with a band you can use to complete 12-15 reps per exercise comfortably. As you progress, you can use thicker bands that offer more resistance.

Execution:

- Band Pull-Aparts: Hold a resistance band with both hands in front of you at chest height. Until your arms are completely stretched to your sides, pull the band outward horizontally. Return to the beginning slowly and repeat. The upper back and shoulders are worked with this workout.
- Squats with Band: Place your feet shoulder-width apart and stand on a resistance band, both hands grasping the band at shoulder height. Maintain the band's tension while you squat. Reposition yourself to the beginning position and continue. This exercises the lower back and legs.
- Chest Press: Secure the band with something hard, like a door handle, behind you. Hold the ends in each hand at chest level with your elbows bent. Return to the starting position carefully after extending your arms with your hands. The chest muscles are the focus of this workout.
- Leg Presses: Place a band around your feet while lying on your back.
- Bend your knees and pull them toward your chest, then extend your legs fully while keeping tension on the band. This targets the quadriceps, hamstrings, and glutes.
- Cool Down: End your workout with 5-10 minutes of static stretching to relax your muscles and improve flexibility.

Focus on stretches that elongate the muscles you've worked during your session.

Benefits

- Enhanced Muscle Strength: Regular use of resistance bands helps in increasing muscle mass and strength by creating tension that muscles must work against.
- Improved Joint Health: The low-impact nature of resistance bands makes them ideal for maintaining joint health and mobility.
- Increased Flexibility and Range of Motion: Resistance bands not only build strength but also enhance flexibility, promoting a greater range of motion.
- Convenience: Lightweight and portable, resistance bands can be used at home, while traveling, or even in a park, making them a very convenient tool for regular exercise.
- Safety: Bands provide a controlled motion path, which minimizes the risk of injury commonly associated with heavy lifting.

Equipment Needed

- Resistance Bands: A variety of bands with different levels of resistance.
- Anchor Point: For exercises that require the band to be stationary, such as chest presses or rowing movements.

Leg Squats

Leg squats are a fundamental strength-training exercise that effectively builds lower body strength and supports core stability. This exercise primarily targets the quadriceps, hamstrings, glutes, and lower back muscles. Squats are highly beneficial for women over 50 as they enhance leg strength, improve balance, and contribute to better functional mobility, which is crucial for maintaining independence and preventing falls.

How to Perform

1. Warm-Up: Start with a general warm-up consisting of light cardiovascular activities such as walking or cycling for about 5-10 minutes, followed by dynamic leg stretches to prepare the muscles for squats.
2. Stance: Place your feet shoulder-width apart, or a little more apart. To aid with balance, hold your arms straight out in front of you. You can also put your hands behind your ears or cross your arms over your chest.

Execution

1. Initiate the Move: Sit back with your hips tucked in, as if you were sitting in an imaginary chair, to start. To keep your back in its natural posture, keep your head forward and your chest up.
2. Going Down: Once your thighs are at least parallel to the floor, bend your knees and lower your body. Make certain

that your knees stay in line with your feet and do not extend over your toes.
3. Rising Up: Put some pressure on your heels to go back to your starting position. This part of the movement should engage your glutes and quadriceps.
4. Repetition: Try to complete 3 sets of 10–15 reps. You may add weights for more resistance as you go, or you can up the amount of sets or repetitions.
5. Cool Down: Finish your routine with static stretches focusing on the lower body to help your muscles relax and recover.

Benefits

1. Strengthens Lower Body: The quadriceps, hamstrings, glutes, and calves are among the main lower body muscles that squats help to strengthen.
2. Enhances Core Stability: Performing squats requires balance and coordination, which naturally engages and strengthens the core muscles.
3. Improves Balance and Coordination: Squats are a great way to increase your balance and coordination and lower your chance of falling.
4. Increases Bone Density: Weight-bearing exercises like squats can help raise bone density, which is crucial for avoiding osteoporosis.
5. Boosts Functional Independence: Everyday tasks like lifting things, bending, and climbing stairs require strong legs and a solid core. Squats facilitate extended functional independence by strengthening these capacities.

Equipment Needed

- No Equipment Necessary: Squats are a versatile exercise that can be performed with just your body weight.

- Optional - Weights: For added resistance, you can use dumbbells, a barbell, or kettlebells. Hold weights at your side, shoulder level, or over your shoulders depending on your comfort and experience level.

Leg squats are a foundational exercise that should be incorporated into the fitness regimen of women over 50, due to their extensive health and functional benefits. With regular practice, squats can significantly enhance quality of life by improving mobility, strength, and overall physical health.

Push-Ups

A traditional upper-body workout that tones the muscles in the chest, shoulders, triceps, and core is the push-up. They are highly effective in developing upper body strength and are easily adaptable to accommodate all fitness levels, even those with limited strength or experience. This makes push-ups especially beneficial for women over 50, as they can help maintain muscle tone, support bone health, and improve posture.

How to Perform

1. Warm-Up: Begin with a general upper-body warm-up such as arm circles, shoulder shrugs, and a few minutes of light aerobic activity to get the blood flowing to your muscles.

Positioning

Standard Push-Up:

1. Placing your hands firmly on the ground, little wider than shoulder-width apart, begin in the plank posture. Make sure your back is flat and your feet are together, extending straight down from your head to your heels.
2. To prevent strain on your joints, contract your core and maintain a small bend in your elbows.

Modified Push-Up:

1. Start on all fours with your knees on the floor and your hands broader than your shoulders on the ground. Lift your feet off the ground just a little bit by crossing them.
2. Make sure your body makes a straight line from your head to your knees by keeping your back flat and using your core.

Execution

Lowering Phase: Breathe in and slowly lower your body toward the floor by bending your elbows. Remain erect and refrain from allowing your hips to rise or slump.

Pushing Phase: Breathe out as you raise your body back up to the initial plank posture by pushing through your hands to extend your elbows.

Repetition: Do two to three sets of eight to twelve repetitions. As you get stronger, go to more difficult versions or up the amount of sets and repetitions.

- Cool Down: End your session with stretches for the chest, shoulders, and back to help your muscles recover and reduce soreness.

Benefits

- Strengthens the Upper Body: Regularly performing push-ups builds strength in the chest, shoulders, triceps, and the stabilizing core muscles.
- Improves Posture: Strengthening the upper body helps maintain good posture, which is important for overall body alignment and health.
- Enhances Core Stability: Push-ups involve the core muscles to keep the body stabilized and aligned during the exercise, which improves core strength and stability.
- Increases Bone Density: Push-ups, being a weight-bearing activity, have the potential to lower the risk of osteoporosis by increasing bone density in the upper body and arms.
- Versatile and Adaptable: Push-ups can be performed anywhere and easily modified to increase or decrease difficulty, making them a versatile addition to any fitness regimen.

Equipment Needed

- No Equipment Necessary: Push-ups generally require no equipment and can be performed just using your body weight.

- Optional - Yoga Mat: For comfort, especially when performing knee push-ups, a mat can be used to cushion your knees.

Push-ups are a foundational exercise that not only enhances physical strength but also contributes to better functional daily activities, making them ideal for women over 50 looking to improve their fitness and overall health. Push-ups are an excellent way to improve bone health, muscular strength, and overall body stability in your workout regimen.

Planks

Planks are a powerful core-strengthening exercise that engage not only the abdominal muscles but also the muscles around the back and pelvis. This exercise is particularly beneficial for women over 50 as it helps to improve core stability, reduce back pain, and enhance posture without the high impact and risks associated with more dynamic exercises.

How to Perform

1. Warm-Up: Start with a light cardiovascular warm-up such as walking or a few dynamic stretches that target the spine

and hip flexors to prepare your body for the static tension of a plank.

Positioning:

Standard Forearm Plank:

- Lay on the ground, face down. With your forearms pointing forward and your elbows exactly beneath your shoulders, raise yourself onto your forearms and toes. The line from your shoulders to your ankles should be a straight one.
- Tighten your glutes and squeeze your belly button into your spine to activate your core. Make sure your hips don't droop or jut upward.

Modified Plank:

If the regular plank is too difficult for you to hold at first, you may adjust it by bringing your knees down to the floor. Make sure your core is active and your back stays straight.

Execution:

- Maintain the plank position while breathing evenly. Avoid holding your breath as it can increase blood pressure unnecessarily.
- Start by holding the plank for 20-30 seconds, gradually working your way up to longer durations, such as one minute or more, as your strength improves.
- Cool Down: After completing your planks, do some gentle stretching for the back, hips, and abdominals to relax the muscles and enhance flexibility.

Benefits

- Core Strength and Stability: Planks work several muscle groups simultaneously, including the abdominals, chest, shoulders, back, and legs, contributing to overall core strength and stability.
- Reduces Back Pain: By strengthening the core, planks can help reduce lower back pain, which is a common ailment for women over 50.
- Improves Posture: Strong core muscles are vital for maintaining proper posture. Planks help keep your bones and joints in the correct alignment, reducing wear and tear on the musculoskeletal system.
- Increases Metabolic Rate: Planks are muscle-strengthening exercises that help increase your metabolic rate, not only during the exercise but also throughout the day.
- Enhances Balance and Coordination: Performing planks regularly can improve your balance and coordination by activating your abdominals, which are crucial for stability.

Equipment Needed

- Yoga Mat: Provides cushioning and traction while performing planks on a hard surface.
- Timer: Useful for tracking the duration of your plank hold.

Planks are an excellent low-impact exercise option that provides significant health benefits for women over 50, from strengthening the core to enhancing overall functional fitness. Integrating this exercise into your routine will support your fitness goals, especially in conjunction with other activities like cardiovascular exercises and strength training.

Step Aerobics

The benefits of strength training and aerobic exercise are combined in step aerobics, a dynamic and rhythmic kind of fitness. Using a raised platform (the step), this workout boosts cardiovascular health, enhances lower body strength, and improves coordination and agility. It is particularly suitable for women over 50 as it can be adjusted to various fitness levels and is less jarring on the joints than other high-impact activities.

How to Perform

- Warm-Up: Begin with a 5-10 minute warm-up of light cardio (such as marching in place) and dynamic stretches to prepare your body for the workout.

Setup:

1. Choosing the Right Step: Use a step platform that can be adjusted for height. Beginners should start with a lower height (about 4-6 inches) and increase it as their fitness improves.
2. Positioning: Stand upright with your feet shoulder-width apart, facing the step.

Execution:

- Basic Step: Begin with the step-up from the basics. As you ascend, bring your left foot up to meet your right foot on the platform. Then, descend with your right foot first, then your left. Repeat, changing the leading foot every time.
- Step up to the right corner of the step with your right foot and step down to the left corner (forming a "V") to return to the ground, always stepping with your right foot first. With every set, swap out the leading foot.
- Knee lifts: Take a step forward with your right foot, then raise your knee toward your chest as you bring your left foot up to the step. Lower your right foot first, then your left. Switch up the side-to-side knee lifts.
- Repeater Knee: Before stepping down and swapping feet, swiftly raise your other knee three times with your stride. Cool Down: Conclude your workout with a five to ten-minute cool-down that consists of static stretches to lengthen the muscles you worked throughout the workout and mild cardio to lower your heart rate.

Benefits

- Enhances Cardiovascular Fitness: Regular participation in step aerobics increases heart rate and breathing, strengthening the heart and lungs, and improving overall aerobic fitness.
- Builds Lower Body Strength: The up-and-down motion on the step particularly targets the quadriceps, hamstrings, and calves while engaging the glutes, thus strengthening these key muscle groups.
- Improves Flexibility and Balance: Through dynamic and diverse movements, step aerobics enhances flexibility and balance, which are important for overall mobility, especially as you age.

- Burns Calories: This vigorous exercise may burn a lot of calories, which helps with weight control and maintaining a healthy metabolism.
- Low Impact: Using a step reduces the impact on your joints compared to traditional aerobic exercises done on the floor, making it safer for your knees and ankles.

Equipment Needed

- Aerobic Step Platform: This is the primary equipment used in step aerobics. Platforms of various heights are available depending on the intensity of the workout desired.
- Comfortable Footwear: Wear supportive, comfortable sneakers to provide stability and cushioning for the movements.

Step aerobics is an effective workout for women over 50 looking to maintain or improve their fitness. It offers a balanced approach to cardiovascular health and muscle strengthening, with a variety of routines to keep the exercise engaging and challenging.

Light Jogging

Light jogging is an accessible and effective cardiovascular exercise that enhances aerobic fitness, strengthens the heart, and improves overall endurance. It involves running at a relaxed pace, which is particularly beneficial for women over 50 as it can be adjusted to suit individual fitness levels while being moderately low in impact. Light jogging helps to maintain cardiovascular health, supports weight management, and boosts mood and mental clarity.

How to Perform

1. Warm-Up: Begin with a 5-10 minute warm-up consisting of walking or dynamic stretches that target the legs and

lower back to prepare your body for the impact and motions of jogging.
2. Gear Up: Wear appropriate running shoes that offer good support and cushioning to minimize the impact on joints. Dress in comfortable, breathable fabrics and supportive clothing.

Jogging Technique:

1. Pace: Maintain a light, manageable pace where you can comfortably hold a conversation. This is often referred to as the "talk test" and is a good indicator that your jogging pace is not too strenuous.
2. Form: Keep your posture straight and relaxed. Look ahead, keep your arms loose at your sides, and let them swing naturally. Your feet should land softly on the ground with each step.
3. Breathing: Focus on deep, rhythmic breathing to ensure adequate oxygen flow through your body, which helps increase endurance and prevent fatigue.
4. Duration and Frequency: Start with short durations of about 10-15 minutes if you are a beginner. Gradually increase your time as your endurance improves, aiming for 20-30 minute sessions. Try to incorporate light jogging into your routine about 2-3 times per week.
5. Cool Down: Finish each jogging session with a 5-10 minute cool down period consisting of walking followed by static stretching to relax and elongate the muscles worked during the jog.

Benefits

- Improves Cardiovascular Health: Regular light jogging increases the efficiency of the cardiovascular system, reduces blood pressure, and helps manage cholesterol levels.
- Enhances Respiratory Strength: Jogging helps improve the capacity and efficiency of the lungs, which is vital for maintaining good health as you age.
- Increases Metabolic Rate: Jogging helps to boost your metabolism, which can aid in weight loss and help manage weight more effectively.
- Strengthens Muscles: It strengthens the leg muscles, including the quadriceps, hamstrings, and calves, as well as the core muscles necessary for good posture and balance.
- Boosts Mental Health: Light jogging has been shown to reduce stress, anxiety, and depression, thanks to the release of endorphins, often referred to as the "runner's high."

Equipment Needed

- Running Shoes: Purchase a decent pair of running shoes with sufficient cushioning and support.
- Purchase a decent pair of running shoes with sufficient cushioning and support.
- Light jogging offers numerous health benefits and is a fantastic way for women over 50 to enhance physical and mental health. It can be a joyful, meditative exercise that strengthens the body, boosts cardiovascular health, and elevates mood.

Kettlebell Workouts

Kettlebell workouts combine strength training with cardiovascular and flexibility exercises, making them a highly efficient form of exercise to enhance overall fitness. Utilizing a kettlebell helps engage multiple muscle groups at once, providing a comprehensive workout that improves strength, boosts cardiovascular health, and increases flexibility.

Women over 50 can benefit most from this kind of exercise since it increases metabolic rate, maintains muscle mass, and improves bone density.

How to Perform

1. Warm-Up: Begin with a general warm-up that consists of five to ten minutes of low-intensity aerobic exercise, such jumping jacks or running in place, and then prepare your body for kettlebell movements with dynamic stretches, especially for the thighs, hips, and shoulders.
2. Choosing the Right Kettlebell: Select a kettlebell that is suitable for your strength level. Typically, women might start with a kettlebell between 8 kg to 12 kg (17 lbs to 26 lbs), but this can vary based on individual strength and fitness.

Technique:

1. Kettlebell Swing: With both hands holding the kettlebell in front of your body and your arms dangling, take a stance with your feet shoulder-width apart. To swing the kettlebell between your legs, flex your knees slightly and pivot at the

hips. Then, straighten your legs and raise the kettlebell to your chest. Do this again in a smooth motion.
2. Kettlebell Goblet Squat: Hold the kettlebell close to your chest with both hands, feet just wider than shoulder-width apart. Holding the kettlebell, squat while maintaining your chest up and your back straight. Get back up to your feet and continue.
3. Kettlebell Lunge Press: Perform a forward lunge holding a kettlebell in your right hand. As you lunge forward, lift the kettlebell above your head. Go back to the beginning and repeat the process on the opposite side.
4. Execution Tips: Keep your movements controlled and fluid. Engage your core throughout each exercise to stabilize your body and protect your spine.
5. Cool Down: Complete with a cool-down that consists of five to ten minutes of stretching that targets all of the major muscle groups, especially the ones that were worked hard during the workout.

Benefits

- Enhanced Strength: Regular kettlebell workouts significantly increase muscular strength, particularly in the core, back, legs, and shoulders.
- Improved Cardiovascular Fitness: The dynamic nature of kettlebell exercises, such as swings and snatches, elevates the heart rate and improves cardiovascular endurance.
- Increased Flexibility: Movements like kettlebell windmills and goblet squats enhance flexibility across multiple joints, improving overall range of motion.
- Weight Management: Kettlebell workouts are excellent for burning calories and boosting metabolic rate, both during and after exercise, aiding in effective weight management.

- Bone Health: Weight-bearing exercises like kettlebell training can strengthen bones and help prevent osteoporosis, a significant concern for women over 50.

Equipment Needed

- Kettlebells: One or more kettlebells of appropriate weights for different exercises.
- Exercise Mat: For comfort and safety, especially when doing floor exercises.
- Protective Gear: Gloves and wrist guards to protect hands and wrists.

Kettlebell workouts are versatile and can be adapted to fit the fitness level of any individual, including women over 50. They provide a challenging yet rewarding experience that enhances muscle coordination, strength, cardiovascular health, and flexibility all at once.

Rowing

Combining aerobic and strength training into one smooth action, rowing is a great full-body exercise. Because it is low-impact and less stressful on weight-bearing joints, it is especially helpful for women over 50. It targets the arms, legs, back, and core, among other main muscle groups.

Rowing not only enhances aerobic stamina but also builds muscle strength and endurance without the harsh impact associated with many other exercises.

How to Perform

- Warm-Up: Start with 5-10 minutes of light cardiovascular exercise such as walking or cycling. Follow up with dynamic stretches that focus on the legs, arms, and back to prepare your body for rowing.

Setting Up the Rowing Machine:

- Adjust the Foot Straps: Ensure your feet are snugly fitted in the footrests with the straps tight enough so your feet feel secure.
- Set the Seat: Sit on the rower and slide the seat to make sure when you extend your legs, your knees are slightly bent and not locked.

Rowing Technique:

- The Catch Position: Begin with knees bent and lean slightly forward from your hips, arms extended, holding the handle with an overhand grip.
- The Drive: Push back with your legs first, then pivot backward from the hips once your legs are mostly straight, pulling the handle to just below your ribs.
- The Finish: Lean back slightly, with shoulders behind the hips. Keep the legs extended, and elbows drawn past the body so that the handle is level with the lower ribs.
- The Recovery: Extend your arms until they straighten, then lean from the hips towards your legs, and finally bend your knees to return to the catch position.
- Execution Tips: Maintain a smooth, fluid motion throughout. The drive should be powerful and initiated mostly by your legs, not your arms.

- Cool Down: Slowly decrease the speed at which you are rowing and switch to 5–10 minutes of stretching, with an emphasis on arm, back, and leg flexibility.

Benefits

- Improves Cardiovascular Health: Rowing increases heart rate and lung capacity, improving overall cardiovascular health.
- Enhances Muscle Strength and Tone: Targets upper body, lower body, and core, providing a balanced muscle workout that strengthens and tones.
- Increases Endurance: Regular rowing can increase stamina and endurance, both muscular and cardiovascular.
- Low Impact on Joints: The seated nature of rowing makes it easier on the joints compared to weight-bearing exercises, which is ideal for older adults.
- Boosts Calorie Burning: Rowing burns a significant amount of calories in a short time due to its full-body engagement, aiding in weight management.

Equipment Needed

- Rowing Machine: The primary equipment used, available at most gyms or as a home fitness equipment.
- Comfortable Clothing: Wear form-fitting clothing to avoid getting caught in the rowing machine, and non-slip, supportive footwear.

Rowing is a versatile and comprehensive exercise that is particularly advantageous for older women looking to maintain or improve their physical health. It provides a substantial aerobic workout that also strengthens the muscles, supports joint health, and improves functional endurance and flexibility. Incorporating rowing into your fitness routine can lead to significant health benefits and contribute to a healthier lifestyle.

Dance Aerobics

Dance aerobics combines the rhythmic movements of dance with traditional aerobic exercises to create a dynamic, enjoyable workout. This form of exercise is especially appealing for women over 50 because it not only improves cardiovascular health and increases endurance but also enhances flexibility and overall body coordination in a fun, energetic environment.

Dance aerobics is a flexible approach to preserving physical health since it can be tailored to different fitness levels and incorporate a variety of dance genres.

How to Perform

1. Warm-Up: Begin with a 5-10 minute warm-up consisting of gentle stretching and basic dance moves to gradually increase your heart rate. This might include steps like side taps, gentle hip rolls, or arm swings.

Dance Moves:

1. Basic Step Touch: Start with simple step-touch movements to the beat of the music, which can later be enhanced with arm movements or increased in speed.
2. Grapevine: This traditional cardiovascular workout consists of walking sideways, crossing one foot behind the other, and then stepping sideways again while hopping a little. It can be modified with turns or arm raises for more intensity.
3. Cha-Cha Steps: Add some Latin flair with simple cha-cha steps. Step forward, then quickly step back while incorporating a small, fast "cha-cha-cha" step.
4. Box Step: Mimic stepping into the four corners of a small box. This move can be performed with varying speeds to adjust the intensity.
5. Routine Creation: Combine various moves into sequences that you can perform repeatedly. Most dance aerobics classes are choreographed with sequences that repeat, allowing participants to catch on and perform the routines more vigorously as they become more familiar.
6. Cool Down: Wind down with a slow dance or simple marching in place followed by extensive stretching focusing on all major muscle groups to help your body cool down and reduce stiffness.

Benefits

1. Improves Cardiovascular Health: Regular participation increases heart rate and breathing, strengthening the heart and improving overall aerobic capacity.
2. Enhances Muscular Endurance: Continuous dance movements build endurance in the major muscle groups.
3. Increases Flexibility: The varied dance moves increase joint range of motion and flexibility, which are important for overall mobility.

4. Boosts Mental Health: Dance aerobics can reduce stress, alleviate symptoms of depression, and boost overall mood through energetic and fun routines.
5. Social Interaction: Often conducted in group settings, dance aerobics classes provide a way to meet new people and enhance social interaction, which is beneficial for mental health.

Equipment Needed

6. Appropriate Footwear: Wear supportive dance sneakers or shoes that provide adequate cushioning and have good lateral support to accommodate movement in all directions.
7. Comfortable Clothing: Choose garments that allow for unrestricted movement and are breathable.
8. Water Bottle: Keep hydrated throughout your workout, especially as dance aerobics can be quite vigorous.

Dance aerobics offers an exciting and effective way for women over 50 to enhance their physical health while enjoying the rhythmic excitement of dance. It serves as a comprehensive workout that supports cardiovascular health, increases muscular endurance and flexibility, and promotes social and mental well-being. Incorporating dance aerobics into your fitness regimen can help maintain vitality, improve body function, and enrich your overall quality of life.

Bodyweight Exercises

Bodyweight exercises are fundamental movements that utilize one's own weight to provide resistance against gravity. These exercises are incredibly effective for developing strength, endurance, flexibility, and balance. Because they can be done anywhere, don't require any particular equipment, and are readily adjusted to meet individual fitness levels and limits, they are especially helpful for women over 50. Common bodyweight exercises include lunges, push-ups, and pull-ups, each targeting different muscle groups to provide a comprehensive workout.

How to Perform

1. Warm-Up: To warm up your muscles and joints for exercise, start with five to ten minutes of mild aerobic activity (such brisk walking or light running) and dynamic stretches.

Lunges:

2. Execution: Place your feet together while standing. With both knees bent at a 90-degree angle, take a big stride forward with one leg and drop your body toward the floor. The rear knee should nearly contact the ground, but not quite.
3. In order to go back to where you were before, push off your front leg. Switch up the legs.
4. Benefits: Lunges enhance hip flexor flexibility and balance while strengthening the legs and buttocks.

Push-Ups:

1. Execution: Start in a plank position with your hands slightly wider than shoulder-width apart. Lower your body

to the floor, keeping your elbows close to your body and your core engaged. Push back up to the starting position.
2. Modifications: If standard push-ups are too challenging, begin with knee push-ups or push-ups against a wall.
3. Benefits: Push-ups build upper body strength and core stability, enhancing overall functional fitness.

Pull-Ups:

1. Execution: Grip a pull-up bar with an overhand grip, hands shoulder-width apart. Pull your body up until your chin is over the bar, then lower yourself back down with control.
2. Modifications: Pull-ups can be challenging; start with assisted pull-up machines or resistance bands if needed.
3. Benefits: Pull-ups primarily target the upper back, shoulders, and arms, and are excellent for strengthening the upper body.
4. Cool Down: End your session with a cool-down period that includes static stretching to relax the muscles and enhance flexibility. Focus particularly on the muscle groups that were most engaged during your workout.

Benefits

- Strengthens Major Muscle Groups: Bodyweight exercises increase muscle mass and strength, promoting better metabolism and increasing bone density.
- Improves Cardiovascular Health: When performed in quick succession or as part of a circuit, bodyweight exercises can elevate the heart rate and improve cardiovascular endurance.
- Enhances Flexibility and Balance: Regular practice improves joint flexibility and overall body balance, crucial for injury prevention and daily function.

- Accessible and Convenient: These exercises require no special equipment and can be done anywhere, making them highly accessible for those with busy lifestyles or limited access to the gym.

Equipment Needed

- Pull-Up Bar: For pull-ups, a home pull-up bar can be installed in a doorway.
- Yoga Mat: Optional for comfort during ground exercises like push-ups or when stretching.

Bodyweight exercises offer an efficient, cost-effective way for women over 50 to maintain physical health, improve functional abilities, and enhance quality of life. These exercises provide a solid foundation for physical activity that supports aging with strength and vitality.

Balance Exercises

Balance exercises are crucial for maintaining and improving stability and coordination, particularly as we age. For women over 50, incorporating balance training into regular fitness routines can significantly enhance quality of life by reducing the risk of falls and improving overall physical function. Simple balance exercises such as standing on one leg or performing balance walks are easy to execute, require minimal space, and can be adapted to fit any fitness level.

How to Perform

1. Warm-Up: Start with a general warm-up consisting of light stretching and mobility exercises for about 5-10 minutes to get your muscles and joints ready.

Standing on One Leg:

2. Execution: Stand straight with your feet hip-width apart and arms at your sides. Lift your right foot off the ground, bending the knee and holding your right foot behind you. Hold the position for as long as you can, then switch to the left foot.
3. Variations: For added difficulty, try closing your eyes, extending your leg forward, or using an unstable surface like a foam pad.
4. Benefits: Improves your static balance, strengthens your ankles and hips, and enhances concentration.

Balance Walks:

- Execution: Extend your arms out to your sides to help maintain balance. Walk in a straight line, placing one foot directly in front of the other, heel to toe, for about 20 steps.

- Variations: Perform this exercise on a balance beam, line on the floor, or along a curb to increase difficulty.
- Benefits: Enhances dynamic balance, coordination, and proprioception (body position awareness).
- Cool Down: Conclude your workout with a cool-down phase that includes stretching focusing on the lower body, especially the calves, hamstrings, and hip flexors, to keep the muscles flexible and prevent tightness.

Benefits

- Reduces Risk of Falls: By improving balance and proprioception, these exercises reduce the risk of falls, which is particularly important for older adults.
- Enhances Joint Stability: Balance training strengthens the muscles around crucial joints such as the ankles, knees, and hips, thereby improving stability.
- Improves Coordination: Regular practice enhances overall coordination and agility, helping with daily activities such as walking and climbing stairs.
- Increases Cognitive Function: Challenges to balance can also stimulate brain functions, which are critical for spatial awareness and multitasking abilities.

Equipment Needed

- No Equipment Necessary: Most balance exercises require no special equipment, making them easy to incorporate into any routine.
- Optional - Stability Tools: For added challenge, you might use a balance cushion, balance board, or stability ball.

Balance exercises are an essential component of a well-rounded fitness program, especially for women over 50. They are not only beneficial for improving physical stability and coordination but also play a crucial role in preventing injuries and enhancing daily life activities. Integrating these exercises into regular workouts can lead to significant improvements in mobility and independence as you age.

Gentle Stretching

Gentle stretching is an essential component of any fitness routine, particularly for women over 50. It helps maintain flexibility, reduces the risk of injury, and can improve overall mobility. These stretches are designed to be low-intensity to ease into a range of motion, making them ideal for cooling down after a workout or for performing on their own to maintain flexibility.

How to Perform

1. Warm-Up: Although stretching itself is often part of a warm-up or cool-down, it's important to ensure your muscles are not completely cold before you begin stretching. Start with a few minutes of light walking or arm circles to get the blood flowing.

Stretching Techniques:

1. Neck Stretch: Gently tilt your head towards your shoulder and hold for 15-30 seconds on each side. This stretch can relieve tension in the neck and upper back.
2. Shoulder Stretch: Bring your right arm across your body, holding it with your left arm just below the elbow, and press gently toward your chest. Hold for 15-30 seconds, then switch arms. This is great for the shoulders and upper back.
3. Torso Stretch: Stand with your feet hip-width apart and reach your arms overhead. Lean to one side, holding for 15-30 seconds, then lean to the other side. This stretch targets the obliques and helps improve overall side flexibility.
4. Hamstring Stretch: Sit on the ground with one leg folded in and the other straight out, toe flexed. Lean forward gently over the straight leg, reaching for your toe. Hold for 15-30 seconds, then switch legs. This stretch is excellent for the back of the legs.
5. Calf Stretch: Stand at arm's length from a wall, step one foot back, and press the heel towards the floor. Keep the back leg straight and the front knee slightly bent. Hold for 15-30 seconds, then switch legs. This helps stretch the calf muscles and Achilles tendon.
6. Quadriceps Stretch: While standing, grab your ankle and pull it towards your buttock, keeping your other hand on a wall for balance. Hold for 15-30 seconds, then switch legs.
7. Cool Down: Use gentle stretching as a cool-down routine to gradually reduce heart rate and relax muscles after vigorous activities or as a standalone routine to maintain flexibility.

Benefits

- Improves Flexibility: Regular stretching helps increase the range of motion in joints, which can improve your daily activities and decrease the risk of injuries.
- Enhances Muscular Relaxation: Gentle stretching relieves muscle tension and can reduce pain and discomfort associated with muscle stiffness.
- Promotes Circulation: Stretching increases blood flow to the muscles, which can shorten recovery time and reduce muscle soreness.
- Reduces Stress: The calming effect of stretching can decrease stress and anxiety levels, promoting overall mental well-being.
- Prevents Injury: By maintaining muscle length and flexibility, stretching can prevent injuries that might occur during more intense physical activities.

Equipment Needed

- Yoga Mat: Optional, provides comfort and support on a hard surface.
- Towel or Stretching Strap: Helpful for performing stretches that require holding onto your feet or legs if flexibility is limited.

Gentle stretching is crucial for maintaining flexibility and preventing injury, particularly as we age. By integrating these stretches into your fitness regimen, you can enhance physical health, improve mobility, and maintain an active lifestyle. Regular stretching not only benefits your physical health but also contributes to mental relaxation and stress reduction.

Chair Exercises

Chair exercises are a safe and effective way to enhance mobility and flexibility, especially for those who may experience discomfort or risk with standing workouts, such as women over 50. These exercises can be performed using a simple chair and are designed to improve muscle tone, joint health, and cardiovascular fitness, all while reducing the strain on the body. They are ideal for individuals with limited mobility or for those who spend long periods sitting.

How to Perform

1. Warm-Up: Begin with a seated march in place for 3-5 minutes to increase circulation. Move your arms in rhythm with your legs to engage the upper body.

Seated Leg Lifts:

2. Execution: Sit upright with feet flat on the floor. Slowly lift one leg straight out in front of you, hold for a few seconds, then lower it back down. Repeat 10-15 times per leg.
3. Benefits: Strengthens the thigh muscles and enhances joint flexibility in the knees and hips.

Chair Squats:

1. Execution: Stand in front of the chair with feet hip-width apart. Slowly bend your knees and lower your body towards the chair, lightly touching the seat before standing back up.

2. Benefits: Builds leg and lower back strength and improves balance and stability.

Seated Torso Twists:

1. Execution: Sit upright with feet flat and place your hands behind your head. Gently twist your torso to one side, return to center, and then twist to the other side.
2. Benefits: Improves flexibility in the spine and strengthens the abdominal muscles.

Arm Circles:

1. Execution: Extend your arms out to the sides at shoulder height. Slowly make small circles, gradually increasing the size. Perform for a few minutes, then reverse the direction.
2. Benefits: Enhances shoulder mobility and strengthens the upper back and arms.

Seated Toe Taps:

1. Execution: Sit upright and alternate tapping your toes on the floor, increasing speed as able.
2. Benefits: Improves lower leg strength and cardiovascular health.
3. Cool Down: Finish with static stretches while seated. Include neck stretches, overhead arm stretches, and forward bends to relax and lengthen the muscles worked.

Benefits

- Enhanced Flexibility and Mobility: Regular chair exercises can increase flexibility in the muscles and joints, improving overall mobility and reducing the risk of falls.

- Increased Muscle Strength: These exercises help maintain muscle strength in the upper and lower body, crucial for daily activities.
- Improved Circulation: Chair exercises can boost cardiovascular health and improve blood circulation, which is beneficial for heart health and energy levels.
- Reduced Pain and Stiffness: Regular movement helps decrease joint stiffness and muscle pain, especially beneficial for those with arthritis or other mobility issues.
- Convenient and Accessible: Can be done at home or in the office, making it easy for those with busy schedules to fit in physical activity.

Equipment Needed

- A Stable Chair: Use a sturdy chair without wheels, preferably with a straight back and no arms.

Optional Equipment:

- Resistance Bands: For added resistance during arm exercises or leg stretches.
- Ankle Weights: To increase the intensity of leg lifts or toe taps.

Chair exercises provide a fantastic option for improving health and physical activity without strain, especially suited to older adults or those with physical limitations. They offer a balanced approach to maintaining fitness, enhancing flexibility, and supporting a healthy lifestyle. Incorporating these exercises into your regular routine can help you stay active and independent.

Creating a Balanced Routine

Establishing a balanced exercise routine is essential for individuals over 50, combining various types of workouts to ensure overall fitness and health. This balance helps prevent overtraining a specific set of muscles and ensures all aspects of physical health are addressed—from cardiovascular conditioning and muscle strength to flexibility and balance.

Weekly Exercise Templates

A well-rounded weekly exercise schedule could include a mix of cardiovascular, strength, flexibility, and balance training. Here's a suggested template:

Monday: Strength Training

Start the week with a session focused on strength training. Incorporate exercises that target all major muscle groups using free weights, machines, or bodyweight exercises. Examples include squats, bench presses, rows, and leg presses. Aim for 8-12 repetitions per set and complete 2-3 sets of each exercise.

Tuesday: Cardiovascular Work

Engage in a cardiovascular exercise that you enjoy, such as brisk walking, jogging, cycling, or swimming. Aim for 30-45 minutes at a moderate intensity where you are breathing hard but can still converse.

Wednesday: Flexibility and Balance

Dedicate this day to activities that enhance flexibility and improve balance. A yoga or Tai Chi session can be particularly beneficial, focusing on dynamic movements that stretch the muscles and incorporate poses that challenge balance.

Thursday: Strength Training

Repeat the strength training session similar to Monday but vary the exercises slightly to target the muscles in different ways. This can involve different equipment or changing the order of exercises.

Friday: Cardiovascular Challenges

Introduce intervals in your cardio session today. After a warm-up, alternate between high-intensity bursts (1-2 minutes) and recovery periods (2-3 minutes). This type of training can help boost metabolism and improve cardiovascular health.

Saturday: Active Recovery

Engage in light activity that isn't as structured as previous workouts. This could be a gentle swim, a leisurely bike ride, or a walk in the park. The idea is to move your body without straining it, helping to recover from the week's workouts.

Sunday: Rest

Allow your body to recover fully by taking a complete rest day. Recovery is crucial to prevent injuries and ensure that the body gets enough time to repair and strengthen.

Adjusting Routines to Energy Levels

Adjusting your exercise routine based on your energy levels is crucial, especially for those over 50. Energy levels can vary dramatically due to various factors, including diet, sleep quality, stress levels, and health issues, so being flexible with your exercise regimen is essential.

Listen to Your Body:

Always tune in to how you feel. If you're particularly tired, it might be wise to switch to a high-intensity workout for something less strenuous or even take an extra rest day if needed. Conversely, if you feel energetic, you might add some extra minutes to your cardio session or include another set of strength exercises.

Modify Intensity and Duration:

Adjust the intensity and duration of your exercises depending on your energy. For example, if strength training sessions are leaving you too tired, reduce the weights or the number of sets. Alternatively, you might extend the duration of low-intensity activities like walking or reduce the time but increase the intensity to get the most out of your energetic days.

Incorporate Flexibility:

Allow for flexibility in your routine. If a scheduled morning workout doesn't work out, be open to exercising at a different time of day. Flexibility in planning can help maintain the consistency of your exercise routine without it becoming a burden.

Assess and Adapt:

Regularly assess your routine's effectiveness and how your body is responding. If you consistently feel worn out or fail to see progress, it may be time to consult with a fitness or health professional to revise your routine. Adjustments may include altering the type of exercises performed, the intensity level, or the overall structure of the workout plan.

Creating a balanced exercise routine is not about rigidly sticking to a schedule but about incorporating a variety of exercises that promote different aspects of fitness while also allowing for adjustments based on physical responses and energy levels. By doing so, individuals over 50 can maintain physical vitality, enhance health outcomes, and ensure that exercise remains a beneficial and enjoyable part of their lives.

CHAPTER 5

RECIPE BOOK I - BREAKFASTS AND SNACKS

A balanced diet is crucial, especially for those engaging in intermittent fasting and exercise routines. Breakfasts and snacks provide the foundational energy and nutrients needed to sustain health and activity levels throughout the day. Understanding how to compose these meals effectively can enhance both nutritional intake and overall well-being.

Understanding Meal Composition

Macronutrient Balance:

Achieving the right balance of macronutrients—proteins, fats, and carbohydrates—is essential for optimizing health and energy levels, particularly for women over 50. Each macronutrient plays a unique role:

Proteins are crucial for repairing and building tissues, including muscles weakened by ageing and intensified by exercise. They also aid in hormone production and provide a feeling of satiety, which is especially important during fasting periods.

Fats are vital for hormone health, which is crucial as women age and experience shifts in hormone levels, including decreased estrogen. Healthy fats, such as those from avocados, nuts, seeds, and olive oil, support brain health and cellular integrity.

Carbohydrates provide the primary energy source for the body and brain. Whole grains, fruits, and vegetables supply fiber, which aids digestion and aids in blood sugar regulation, avoiding the spikes and crashes that can occur in diets high in refined sugars.

A well-composed meal should include a mix of these macronutrients to support bodily functions, enhance energy levels throughout the fasting periods, and ensure overall health.

Ideas for Quick and Nutritious Breakfasts

Greek Yogurt Parfait Recipe

Ingredients

- 1 cup Greek yogurt (plain or vanilla)
- 1/2 cup granola (whole grain preferred)
- 1/2 cup mixed berries (strawberries, blueberries, raspberries), fresh or frozen
- 1-2 tablespoons honey
- 1 tablespoon chia seeds

Method

1. Prepare Berries: Wash the berries thoroughly. Hull and slice strawberries if using.

2. 2. Layer Ingredients: - Place a layer of Greek yogurt into the bottom of a glass or bowl.
    a. Add a layer of granola on top of the yogurt.
    b. Continue with a layer of mixed berries.
    c. Repeat the layering process until all ingredients are used, finishing with a layer of berries.
3. Garnish: Drizzle honey over the top berry layer. Sprinkle chia seeds evenly over the honey.
4. Serve: Enjoy immediately for a crunchy texture or refrigerate overnight for a softer muesli-like consistency.

Benefits

- High Protein Content: Greek yogurt provides a high amount of protein, which is essential for muscle repair and growth, and helps keep you feeling full longer.
- Rich in Antioxidants: Berries are high in antioxidants, which help combat oxidative stress and inflammation in the body.
- Fiber Boost: The combination of berries, granola, and chia seeds adds a good amount of fiber, which promotes digestive health and satiety.
- Omega-3 Fatty Acids: Chia seeds are a great source of omega-3 fatty acids, which are important for brain health and reducing inflammation.
- Energy Providing: The natural sugars in honey paired with fiber and protein provide a balanced release of energy, making this parfait a great way to start the day.

This Greek Yogurt Parfait is not only delicious but also packs a nutritional punch that supports overall health and energy levels, making it an ideal breakfast or snack option.

Spinach and Mushroom Omelets

Ingredients

- 3 large eggs
- 1 cup fresh spinach, roughly chopped
- 1/2 cup mushrooms, sliced
- 1/4 cup onions, finely chopped
- 2 tablespoons olive oil
- 1/4 cup low-fat cheese (cheddar or mozzarella), shredded
- Salt and pepper, to taste

Method

1. Prepare Vegetables:
    - Heat one tablespoon of olive oil in a non-stick skillet over medium heat.
    - Add the chopped onions and sliced mushrooms to the skillet. Sauté for 5-7 minutes until the mushrooms are browned and onions are translucent.

- Add the chopped spinach to the skillet. Cook for an additional 2-3 minutes until the spinach is wilted. Remove the vegetables from the skillet and set aside.
2. Cook the Omelet:
   - In a bowl, beat the eggs with a pinch of salt and pepper until well combined.
   - Heat the remaining tablespoon of olive oil in the same skillet over medium heat.
   - Pour the beaten eggs into the skillet, ensuring they spread evenly across the bottom.
   - As the eggs begin to set, spoon the sautéed vegetables evenly over one half of the eggs.
   - Sprinkle the shredded cheese over the vegetables.
3. Fold and Serve:
   - Once the eggs are fully set and the bottom is golden brown, carefully fold the omelet in half, covering the vegetables with the other side of the egg.
   - Let the omelet cook for another minute to ensure the cheese melts.
   - Carefully slide the omelet onto a plate and serve hot.

Benefits

- High-Quality Protein: Eggs provide a high-quality source of protein, which is essential for muscle repair, immune function, and overall health.
- Nutrient-Rich Vegetables: Spinach and mushrooms contribute a variety of essential vitamins and minerals, such as iron, vitamin C, and potassium, which support heart health and immune function.

- Healthy Fats: Olive oil and cheese add healthy fats to the omelet, which help enhance satiety and provide a sustained source of energy.
- Dietary Fiber: Vegetables like onions and spinach also add fiber to the meal, promoting digestive health and further aiding in satiety.

This Spinach and Mushroom Omelet is a nutritious, fulfilling meal that combines the rich flavors of sautéed vegetables with the hearty texture of eggs and cheese. It's perfect for a healthful breakfast or a light dinner, providing a balanced mix of proteins, healthy fats, and essential nutrients.

Smoothie Bowl:

Ingredients

- 2 frozen bananas, sliced
- 1 cup mixed berries (such as blueberries, raspberries, and strawberries), frozen
- 1 cup fresh spinach
- 1 scoop protein powder (any flavor that complements berries, typically vanilla or unflavored)
- 1 cup almond milk (unsweetened)
-

Toppings:

- 2 tablespoons sliced almonds
- 2 tablespoons coconut flakes
- Additional fresh berries for garnish

Method

Blend the Smoothie:

- In a high-powered blender, combine the frozen bananas, mixed berries, fresh spinach, protein powder, and almond milk.
- Blend on high speed until the mixture is completely smooth and creamy. Adjust the consistency by adding a little more almond milk if the mixture is too thick.

Assemble the Bowl:

- Pour the smoothie mixture into a deep bowl.
- Arrange the sliced almonds, coconut flakes, and fresh berries on top of the smoothie mixture in a neat, appealing pattern.

Serve:

- Enjoy immediately while it's cold and fresh for the best texture and flavor.

Benefits

- Rich in Dietary Fiber: Both fruits and spinach provide a good amount of dietary fiber, which helps in regulating digestion and maintaining low blood sugar levels.
- High in Vitamins and Minerals: The fruits and spinach in this smoothie bowl are high in vitamins such as Vitamin C and A, along with minerals like iron and magnesium, which are crucial for overall health.
- Protein for Muscle Repair: The addition of protein powder makes this bowl a great post-workout option, helping to repair muscles and stave off hunger.

- Healthy Fats: Toppings like almonds and coconut flakes offer healthy fats that are good for heart health and help to keep you satiated.

This smoothie bowl is not only a delicious, refreshing breakfast or snack but also a nutritional powerhouse that supports overall health with essential fibers, proteins, and healthy fats. Perfect for a quick meal, it ensures you start your day loaded with nutrients without compromising on taste.

Avocado Toast with Egg:

Ingredients

- 2 slices whole-grain bread
- 1 ripe avocado
- 2 eggs
- 1/2 cup cherry tomatoes, halved
- Salt, to taste
- Black pepper, to taste
- Crushed red pepper flakes, to taste

Method

Prepare the Toast:

1. Toast the whole-grain bread slices to your desired crispness in a toaster or on a skillet over medium heat.
2. Mash the Avocado:
3. While the bread is toasting, cut the avocado in half, remove the pit, and scoop the flesh into a small bowl.
4. Mash the avocado with a fork until it reaches a smooth consistency. Season with salt and pepper to taste.

Cook the Eggs:

5. Heat a non-stick skillet over medium heat and lightly oil it if desired.
6. Crack the eggs into the skillet and cook according to preference: for sunny side up, let the eggs cook until the whites are set but the yolks remain runny; for over-easy, flip the eggs over after the whites set and cook for an additional minute.

Assemble the Avocado Toast:

7. Spread the mashed avocado evenly over each slice of toasted bread.
8. Carefully place a cooked egg on top of each avocado-smeared toast.
9. Sprinkle crushed red pepper flakes over the eggs for a bit of spice.

Add the Tomatoes:

10. Serve the avocado toast with a side of fresh halved cherry tomatoes.

Benefits

- Healthy Fats: Avocado is rich in monounsaturated fats that are beneficial for heart health and help maintain good cholesterol levels.
- High-Quality Protein: The egg provides a complete protein, containing all nine essential amino acids necessary for bodily repair and muscle growth.
- Complex Carbohydrates: Whole-grain bread supplies sustained energy through complex carbohydrates which also aid in digestion due to their high fiber content.

- Rich in Vitamins and Minerals: Cherry tomatoes add a nutritional boost with vitamin C, potassium, and other antioxidants.

This Avocado Toast with Egg is a nutritious, filling meal that combines healthy fats, proteins, and complex carbohydrates, making it an ideal choice for breakfast or a light lunch. It's simple to prepare and can be customized with various toppings according to your taste preferences and dietary needs.

5. Nut Butter and Banana Sandwich:

Ingredients

- 2 slices of whole-grain bread
- 2 tablespoons almond butter or peanut butter
- 1 medium banana, sliced
- A dash of cinnamon

Method

1. Lightly toast the whole-grain bread slices if preferred for added texture and flavor.
2. Spread one tablespoon of almond or peanut butter evenly on each slice of bread.
3. Arrange the banana slices over one slice of bread, completely covering the nut butter layer.
4. Sprinkle a dash of cinnamon over the banana slices.
5. Place the second slice of bread, nut butter side down, on top of the banana slices to form the sandwich.

6. Cut the sandwich in half or quarters and serve immediately.

Benefits

- Nut butter provides essential proteins and healthy fats that promote tissue repair and satiety.
- Bananas offer quick-releasing energy and are rich in potassium, which supports heart health and muscle function.
- Whole-grain bread contributes dietary fiber, aiding digestion and prolonging fullness, ideal for sustained energy release during fasting periods.

This Nut Butter and Banana Sandwich is quick and easy to prepare, making it a perfect, balanced meal for breakfast or a nutritious snack, providing a good mix of macronutrients to support overall health and energy levels throughout the day.

Vegetarian Breakfast Recipes

For those following a vegetarian diet, breakfast can be both delicious and nutritious, setting the tone for a day of healthy eating. Vegetarian breakfasts can easily incorporate a balanced mix of macronutrients—proteins, fats, and carbohydrates—to sustain energy levels, support metabolic health, and provide essential nutrients. Here, we explore some appealing vegetarian breakfast recipes, focusing on smoothies, bowls, and hearty oatmeal options.

Smoothies and Bowls

Ingredients

- 1 cup fresh spinach
- 1 ripe banana
- ½ avocado
- 1 tablespoon chia seeds
- 1 scoop protein powder (plant-based)
- 1 cup unsweetened almond milk
- A few ice cubes

Method

1. Place the spinach, banana, avocado, chia seeds, protein powder, almond milk, and ice cubes into a blender.
2. Blend on high until all components are completely smooth.
3. Check the consistency; if the smoothie is too thick, add a bit more almond milk and blend again to achieve the desired thickness.

Benefits

- Protein Rich: The plant-based protein powder and chia seeds provide high-quality protein essential for muscle repair and growth.
- Fiber Content: Spinach and avocado are excellent sources of fiber, which promotes digestive health and satiety.
- Healthy Fats: Avocado includes healthy monounsaturated fats, which are beneficial for heart health and overall well-being.
- Vitamins and Minerals: This smoothie is packed with a variety of vitamins and minerals from spinach and avocado, enhancing overall nutrient intake.

This Green Protein Smoothie is not only nourishing but also delicious, making it a perfect meal replacement or post-workout drink to support muscle recovery and provide vital nutrients for daily activities.

Berry Almond Breakfast Bowl

Oatmeal with Almond Butter and Berries

Ingredients

- ½ cup rolled oats
- 1 cup almond milk
- 1 tablespoon flaxseed meal
- ½ teaspoon vanilla extract
- ½ cup mixed berries (fresh or frozen)
- 1 tablespoon almond butter
- A few almonds, chopped

- A sprinkle of cinnamon

Method

1. In a small saucepan, combine the rolled oats, almond milk, flaxseed meal, and vanilla extract.
2. Cook over medium heat, stirring occasionally, until the oats are soft and have absorbed most of the almond milk. This typically takes about 5 to 7 minutes.
3. Once cooked, pour the oat mixture into a serving bowl.
4. Top the oatmeal with mixed berries, a dollop of almond butter, and a few chopped almonds.
5. Finish with a sprinkle of cinnamon for added flavor.

Benefits

- Dietary Fiber: Both oats and flaxseed are excellent sources of fiber, which aids in digestion and helps maintain a healthy gut.
- Protein and Healthy Fats: Almond butter and almonds provide good amounts of protein and healthy monounsaturated fats, which promote satiety and are beneficial for heart health.
- Antioxidants: Berries are rich in antioxidants, which help combat oxidative stress and inflammation in the body.
- Overall Nutritional Balance: This meal offers a balanced blend of macronutrients, making it an ideal breakfast option that provides sustained energy and keeps you feeling full longer.

This wholesome oatmeal recipe is not only hearty and satisfying but also packs a nutritional punch, making it a perfect breakfast to start an active day. The combination of flavors and textures from the creamy oats, juicy berries, rich almond butter, and crunchy almonds ensures that this meal is as delicious as it is healthy.

Savory Oatmeal with Grated Zucchini and Mushrooms

Ingredients

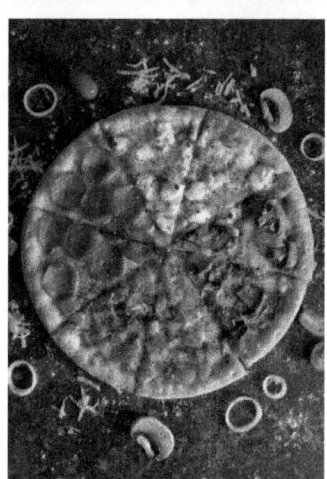

- ½ cup rolled oats
- 1 cup vegetable broth or water
- ½ cup grated zucchini
- ½ cup sliced mushrooms
- 1 tablespoon nutritional yeast
- A pinch of salt and pepper
- 1 teaspoon olive oil

Method

1. Heat the olive oil in a pan over medium heat. Add the sliced mushrooms and sauté until they are golden and tender.
2. To the pan, add the rolled oats and grated zucchini. Stir to mix.
3. Pour in the vegetable broth (or water) and bring the mixture to a simmer. Cook for about 7-10 minutes, or until the oats are tender and have absorbed most of the liquid.
4. Remove from heat and stir in the nutritional yeast, salt, and pepper until well combined.

Benefits

1. Whole Grains: Rolled oats are a great source of complex carbohydrates and fiber, which aid in digestion and provide sustained energy.
2. Vegetables: Zucchini and mushrooms not only add flavor and texture but also include important vitamins and minerals that enhance overall health.

3. **Nutritional Yeast:** This ingredient is rich in B vitamins, particularly B12, making it a valuable addition to vegetarian diets where B12 can be lacking. It also adds a cheesy flavor without the dairy.
4. **Healthy Fats:** Olive oil provides monounsaturated fats, beneficial for heart health.
5. **Protein and Fiber:** The combination of oats, vegetables, and nutritional yeast delivers a good balance of protein and fiber, making this dish particularly satisfying and good for maintaining healthy blood sugar levels.

This savory oatmeal recipe offers a delicious twist on traditional breakfast porridge, providing a nutrient-rich, balanced meal that satisfies with its deep umami flavors and hearty texture. Perfect for a warming breakfast or a cozy dinner, it's a versatile dish that supports a healthy diet.

Chia and Hemp Seed Pudding Recipe

Ingredients

- 3 tablespoons chia seeds
- 1 tablespoon hemp seeds
- 1 cup coconut milk
- 1 tablespoon maple syrup
- ½ teaspoon vanilla extract

Method

1. In a bowl or a mason jar, combine the chia seeds, hemp seeds, coconut milk, maple syrup, and vanilla extract.

2. Mix all the ingredients thoroughly to ensure the chia seeds do not clump together.
3. Cover the mixture and refrigerate overnight to allow the chia seeds to absorb the coconut milk and expand, creating a pudding-like consistency.
4. In the morning, give the pudding a good stir to break up any clumps and check the consistency. If it's too thick, you can adjust by adding a bit more coconut milk.
5. Serve the pudding with a topping of your choice such as fresh fruits, nuts, or a sprinkle of cinnamon for extra flavor.

Benefits

1. Plant-Based Protein: Chia and hemp seeds both provide high-quality plant-based protein which is essential for muscle repair and growth.
2. Omega-3 Fatty Acids: These seeds are rich in omega-3 fatty acids, known for their anti-inflammatory properties and benefits to heart health.
3. Healthy Fats: Coconut milk is a great source of medium-chain triglycerides (MCTs), healthy fats that can help boost metabolism and provide sustained energy.
4. Dietary Fiber: Chia seeds are a fantastic source of fiber, which promotes digestive health and can aid in maintaining healthy blood sugar levels.
5. Versatile and Nutrient-Dense: This pudding is not only filling and satisfying but also packed with nutrients that support overall health, making it an ideal breakfast or snack option.

This Chia and Hemp Seed Pudding is an easy, nutritious recipe perfect for busy mornings or as a healthy dessert option. Its rich texture and versatility in toppings make it a delicious treat that benefits overall wellness.

Whole Wheat Vegetable Muffins Recipe

Ingredients

- 1 cup whole wheat flour
- 1 teaspoon baking powder
- 2 eggs
- ¼ cup olive oil
- ½ cup unsweetened almond milk
- ½ cup chopped spinach
- ½ cup diced tomatoes
- ¼ cup grated cheese (optional)
- Salt and pepper, to taste

Method

1. Preheat Oven: Set your oven to 375°F (190°C). Lightly grease or line a muffin tin with paper liners.
2. Mix Dry Ingredients: In a large mixing bowl, sift together the whole wheat flour and baking powder. This ensures your baking powder is evenly distributed throughout the flour.
3. Combine Wet Ingredients: In another bowl, whisk together the eggs, olive oil, and almond milk until the mixture is smooth.
4. Combine Wet and Dry Ingredients: Gradually add the wet ingredients to the dry ingredients, stirring just until combined. It's important not to overmix to keep the muffins light and fluffy.
5. Add Vegetables and Cheese: Fold in the chopped spinach, diced tomatoes, and grated cheese into the batter. Season with salt and pepper to taste.

6. Bake: Spoon the batter into the prepared muffin tins, filling each cup about three-quarters full. Bake in the preheated oven for 20-25 minutes, or until the tops are golden and a toothpick inserted into the center of a muffin comes out clean.
7. Cool and Serve: Allow the muffins to cool in the pan for a few minutes before transferring them to a wire rack to cool completely. Serve warm or at room temperature.

Benefits

- Balanced Nutrition: These muffins provide a well-rounded balance of carbohydrates, protein, and healthy fats. Whole wheat flour offers more fiber than refined flours, which aids in digestion and provides longer-lasting energy.
- Rich in Vitamins and Minerals: Spinach and tomatoes add essential nutrients, including iron, vitamin C, and potassium, which are crucial for health and well-being.
- Heart-Healthy Fats: Olive oil is a good source of monounsaturated fats, which are beneficial for heart health.
- Protein Boost: Eggs and cheese (if used) add high-quality protein, which is essential for muscle repair and growth.
- Convenience: These muffins are easy to make, portable, and perfect for on-the-go breakfasts or snacks.

These Whole Wheat Vegetable Muffins are not just tasty but also incredibly nutritious, making them a perfect start to the day, especially for those following a vegetarian diet. They complement an intermittent fasting regimen by providing sustained energy through balanced macronutrients. Enjoy them fresh for breakfast or as a quick snack throughout your busy day!

Non-Vegetarian Breakfast Recipes

Non-vegetarian breakfast options provide a fantastic way to incorporate high-quality protein and essential nutrients that support an active lifestyle and complement intermittent fasting. Protein-rich starters and various egg-based dishes can deliver sustained energy and critical amino acids, which are vital for muscle repair, cognitive function, and overall health maintenance.

Smoked Salmon and Cream Cheese Bagel

Ingredients

- 1 whole grain bagel
- 2 ounces smoked salmon
- 2 tablespoons cream cheese
- 1 tablespoon capers
- Slices of red onion
- Fresh dill for garnish

Method

1. Toast the Bagel: Cut the whole grain bagel in half and toast it to your preference.
2. Spread Cream Cheese: Once toasted, spread the cream cheese evenly on both halves of the bagel.

3. Add Smoked Salmon: Lay the slices of smoked salmon over the cream cheese on each bagel half.

4. Garnish: Sprinkle capers over the smoked salmon. Add a few slices of red onion and garnish with fresh dill to enhance the flavor.

Benefits

- Omega-3 Fatty Acids: Smoked salmon is a great source of omega-3 fatty acids, which are crucial for cardiovascular health and can help reduce inflammation throughout the body.
- Rich in Protein: Salmon not only provides essential omega-3s but is also a rich source of high-quality protein that aids in muscle repair and growth.
- Dietary Fiber: The whole grain bagel adds a healthy dose of fiber, which promotes digestive health and helps to stabilize blood sugar levels.
- Flavorful and Satisfying: This meal not only satisfies taste buds with its rich flavors but also provides a balanced mix of nutrients, making it a wholesome choice for any meal of the day.

This Smoked Salmon and Cream Cheese Bagel combines simplicity with gourmet appeal, making it a luxurious yet easy-to-prepare dish that's perfect for breakfast, brunch, or a light meal. Enjoy the harmonious blend of flavors and the nutritional benefits it brings, especially good for those seeking heart-healthy options.

Greek Yogurt with Honey and Nuts

Ingredients

- 1 cup Greek yogurt
- 2 tablespoons honey
- 1/4 cup mixed nuts (almonds, walnuts, and pecans), roughly chopped

- A sprinkle of cinnamon

Method

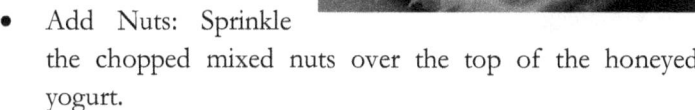

- Prepare the Yogurt: Place the Greek yogurt in a serving bowl.
- Add Honey: Drizzle the honey evenly over the yogurt.
- Add Nuts: Sprinkle the chopped mixed nuts over the top of the honeyed yogurt.
- Garnish: Lightly dust the top with cinnamon for added flavor.

Benefits

- High in Protein: Greek yogurt is rich in protein, which is essential for muscle repair and growth, and helps keep you feeling full longer.
- Digestive Health: The probiotics found in Greek yogurt help enhance the digestive system's health by balancing the gut microbiota.
- Healthy Fats: Nuts provide healthy monounsaturated and polyunsaturated fats, which are crucial for heart health and can help maintain normal blood cholesterol levels.
- Additional Nutrients: Nuts are also a good source of fiber, antioxidants, and vitamins such as Vitamin E and magnesium, enhancing this dish's nutritional profile.
- Energy Boosting: The combination of protein from the yogurt and healthy fats from the nuts provides sustained energy, making it an excellent start to the day.

This Greek Yogurt with Honey and Nuts is not only delicious but also packs a substantial nutritional punch. It's a quick and easy breakfast option that effectively balances good taste with health benefits, making it an ideal morning treat that supports an active lifestyle and complements an intermittent fasting regimen.

Eggs Various Ways

Classic Omelet with Spinach and Feta

Ingredients

- 3 eggs
- 1/2 cup chopped spinach
- 1/4 cup crumbled feta cheese
- Salt, to taste
- Pepper, to taste
- 1 teaspoon olive oil

Method

1. Beat the Eggs: Crack the eggs into a mixing bowl. Add salt and pepper to taste, and beat well until the mixture is smooth and uniform.
2. Prepare the Skillet: Heat the olive oil in a skillet over medium heat. Ensure the oil is spread evenly across the bottom of the skillet.
3. Cook the Eggs: Pour the beaten eggs into the skillet. Let them sit undisturbed for a minute until they start to set around the edges.
4. Add Fillings: Sprinkle the chopped spinach and crumbled feta cheese evenly over the eggs. Allow the eggs to continue cooking until they are mostly set but still slightly runny on top.

5. Fold the Omelet: Carefully fold the omelet in half using a spatula, enclosing the spinach and feta filling. Continue cooking for another minute or two until the omelet is fully set and the feta cheese begins to melt.
6. Finish and Serve: Gently slide the omelet onto a plate. The omelet can be cut in half if serving two. Serve hot for the best flavor and texture.

Benefits

- Complete Protein Source: Eggs provide high-quality protein with all essential amino acids, making them excellent for muscle repair and growth.
- Rich in Iron and Vitamins: Spinach is loaded with iron and vitamins A and C, which are crucial for maintaining healthy skin, hair, and immune system.
- Calcium-Rich: Feta cheese offers a significant amount of calcium, which is essential for strong bones and teeth.
- Healthy Fats: Olive oil contains monounsaturated fats, which are known to be heart-healthy and beneficial for cholesterol levels.

This Classic Omelet with Spinach and Feta is a delicious, nutritious meal that combines the fluffy texture of eggs with the rich flavors of spinach and feta. It's an easy-to-make breakfast or brunch option that delivers a balanced mix of proteins, vitamins, and minerals, enhancing your diet while providing a satisfying and tasty meal.

Sunny-Side Up Eggs on Avocado Toast

Ingredients

- 2 eggs
- 2 slices of whole-grain bread
- 1 ripe avocado
- Lemon juice (to taste)
- Salt (to taste)
- Pepper (to taste)

Method

1. Toast the Bread: Place the whole-grain bread slices in a toaster or on a skillet over medium heat. Toast until they are golden and crispy.
2. Prepare Avocado Spread:
3. Cut the avocado in half, remove the pit, and scoop the flesh into a small bowl.
4. Mash the avocado with a fork until it reaches a creamy consistency.
5. Add lemon juice, salt, and pepper to the mashed avocado according to taste. Mix well.

Cook the Eggs:

1. Heat a non-stick skillet over medium heat. You can add a small amount of oil or butter to prevent sticking if desired.
2. Crack the eggs into the skillet, taking care not to break the yolks. Cook until the whites are firmly set but the yolks remain runny, about 3-4 minutes. Season with salt and pepper during cooking.

Assemble the Toast:

- Spread the mashed avocado evenly on each slice of toasted bread.
- Carefully place a cooked sunny-side up egg on top of each avocado spread.

Benefits

- Balanced Macronutrients: This meal provides a perfect balance of proteins, fats, and carbohydrates. The proteins and healthy fats help promote satiety and are essential for various bodily functions.
- Heart-Healthy Fats: Avocado is rich in monounsaturated fats, which are beneficial for heart health and help reduce bad cholesterol levels.
- High-Quality Protein: Eggs are a complete protein source, providing all essential amino acids needed for muscle repair and overall health.
- Fiber-Rich: Whole-grain bread offers a good source of dietary fiber, which aids in digestion and helps maintain steady blood sugar levels.

This Avocado Toast with Sunny-Side Up Eggs is not only a visually appealing dish but also combines nutrient-dense ingredients to create a delicious and satisfying meal. It's perfect for a hearty breakfast or a wholesome brunch that will keep you fueled and content throughout the day.

Breakfast Burrito with Sausage and Beans

Ingredients

- 2 whole wheat tortillas
- 4 ounces ground turkey sausage

- 1/2 cup canned black beans, rinsed and drained
- 1/2 cup diced tomatoes
- 1/4 cup shredded cheese (choice of cheddar, Monterey Jack, etc.)
- 2 eggs
- Salsa for serving

Method

1. Cook Sausage: In a skillet over medium heat, cook the turkey sausage until it's browned and no longer pink, breaking it up into small pieces as it cooks.
2. Scramble Eggs: Once the sausage is cooked, crack the eggs directly into the skillet with the sausage. Stir and scramble the eggs with the sausage until the eggs are fully cooked.
3. Prepare Tortillas: Warm the whole wheat tortillas in another skillet or microwave for about 10-15 seconds to make them pliable and warm.

Assemble Burritos:

1. Lay the warm tortillas on a clean flat surface.

2. Evenly distribute the sausage and egg mixture down the center of each tortilla.
3. Top the mixture with black beans, diced tomatoes, and shredded cheese.
4. Roll Burritos: Fold in the sides of the tortilla and roll it up tightly to enclose the filling. Ensure the edges are tucked in to hold the ingredients inside.
5. Serve: Cut each burrito in half, if desired, and serve with salsa on the side.

Benefits

1. Lean Protein: Turkey sausage is a great source of lean protein which helps in muscle repair and growth. It's a healthier alternative to traditional pork sausage, offering similar flavors but with less fat.
2. Fiber and Protein: Black beans are not only high in protein but also a good source of fiber, which helps in digestion and provides a feeling of fullness.
3. Nutrient-Dense: Tomatoes add a healthy dose of vitamins A and C, which are antioxidants that help in immune function and skin health.
4. Whole Grains: Whole wheat tortillas provide complex carbohydrates and fibers that are essential for sustained energy throughout the day.
5. Calcium and Fats: Cheese adds calcium for bone health and fats for taste and additional satiety.

This Breakfast Burrito with Sausage and Beans is a nutritious, satisfying meal that is perfect for a hearty breakfast. It combines flavorful, protein-rich ingredients in a convenient and portable form, making it ideal for a quick breakfast on the go or a leisurely brunch at home. Its balanced content of macronutrients ensures that you start your day with the energy you need.

These non-vegetarian breakfast recipes are designed to cater to various tastes and dietary preferences while ensuring a high-protein start to the day. They support muscle maintenance and metabolic health and provide the necessary energy and nutrients for those practicing intermittent fasting and engaging in regular physical activity. Whether you prefer simple eggs on toast or a more elaborate smoked salmon bagel, these recipes ensure a delicious, nutritious beginning to any day.

Healthy Snacks

Healthy snacks are an integral part of any diet, especially for those incorporating intermittent fasting and rigorous exercise routines. They not only stave off hunger between meals but also provide vital nutrients and energy boosts without excessive calorie intake. Here, we explore both energy-boosting bites and low-calorie options that are perfect for maintaining energy levels and supporting a healthy metabolism.

Almond and Date Energy Balls

Ingredients

- 1 cup pitted dates
- 1 cup almonds
- 1/4 cup shredded coconut
- 1 tablespoon chia seeds
- 1 tablespoon flax seeds
- A pinch of salt

Method

1. Blend Dates and Almonds: Place the pitted dates and almonds in a food processor. Blend until the mixture forms a sticky dough. You may need to stop occasionally to push the mixture down the sides of the processor bowl to ensure even blending.
2. Add Seeds and Coconut: To the sticky dough in the food processor, add the chia seeds, flax seeds, shredded coconut, and a pinch of salt. Pulse the processor several times until all ingredients are well combined and the mixture is uniform.
3. Form Energy Balls: Take small portions of the mixture and roll them into balls about the size of a walnut. If the mixture is too sticky, wet your hands slightly with water to help prevent sticking.
4. Chill: Place the rolled energy balls on a baking sheet or plate lined with parchment paper. Refrigerate the balls for at least an hour to set and firm up.

Benefits

- Quick Energy Source: Dates are rich in natural sugars, making these energy balls a great source of quick energy, which is perfect for pre or post-workout snacks.
- Protein and Healthy Fats: Almonds provide a substantial amount of protein and healthy monounsaturated fats, which are essential for muscle repair and overall health.
- Omega-3 Fatty Acids: Both chia and flax seeds are excellent sources of omega-3 fatty acids, which contribute to cardiovascular health and reduce inflammation.
- Fiber: The high fiber content in these ingredients helps to promote digestive health and keep you feeling full longer, aiding in weight management.

These Almond and Date Energy Balls are not only delicious but also incredibly nourishing. They make for a convenient and healthy snack that can easily be taken on the go, providing a perfect blend of essential nutrients and energy whenever you need a quick boost.

Greek Yogurt and Mixed Berries

Ingredients

- 1 cup Greek yogurt
- 1/2 cup mixed berries (blueberries, raspberries, strawberries)
- A drizzle of honey

Method

1. Prepare Berries: Wash the berries thoroughly and pat them dry. If the strawberries are large, slice them into smaller pieces to match the size of the blueberries and raspberries.
2. Assemble the Dish: Scoop the Greek yogurt into a bowl. Top with the mixed berries evenly distributed over the yogurt.
3. Add Sweetness: Drizzle honey over the berries and yogurt to enhance the flavors and add a touch of sweetness.

Benefits

- High in Protein: Greek yogurt provides a robust amount of protein, which is crucial for muscle repair and growth.
- Digestive Health Support: The probiotics in Greek yogurt help maintain a healthy balance in the gut microbiome, aiding in digestion and overall gastrointestinal health.

- Antioxidant-Rich Berries: Berries are loaded with antioxidants that help combat oxidative stress and inflammation in the body.
- Natural Sugars and Fiber: Berries offer a healthy dose of natural sugars for energy, along with fiber, which helps moderate blood sugar levels and promotes satiety.

This Greek Yogurt and Mixed Berries dish is an excellent, quick, and easy breakfast or snack option that is not only delicious but also highly nutritious. It combines the creamy texture of yogurt with the fresh zest of berries, all sweetened naturally with honey, making it a perfect meal to boost your energy and support your health.

Peanut Butter Banana Smoothie:

Ingredients

- 1 banana
- 2 tablespoons peanut butter
- 1 cup almond milk
- 1 teaspoon honey
- A handful of ice cubes

Method

1. Combine Ingredients: In a blender, add the banana (sliced for easier blending), peanut butter, almond milk, honey, and ice cubes.
2. Blend: Blend on high speed until all components are thoroughly combined and the mixture is smooth. Ensure there are no lumps of peanut butter or banana left.

3. Adjust Consistency: If the smoothie is too thick, gradually add more almond milk and blend again to reach the desired consistency.
4. Serve: Pour the smoothie into a glass and serve immediately for the freshest taste and best texture.

Benefits

1. Energy Boosting: Bananas provide a quick release of natural sugars, offering an immediate energy boost.
2. Sustained Energy: Peanut butter is rich in protein and healthy fats, which help in maintaining long-lasting energy levels, making this smoothie a perfect snack to stave off hunger between meals.
3. Healthy Fats: Peanut butter and almond milk contribute healthy fats that are good for heart health and can help to stabilize blood sugar levels.
4. Nutrient Rich: This smoothie also packs vitamins such as Vitamin E from almond milk and a host of B vitamins from banana, which are essential for energy metabolism and overall health.

This Banana and Peanut Butter Smoothie is not only delicious but also incredibly nourishing, making it an ideal choice for a quick breakfast or a wholesome snack. It's easy to make and can be a satisfying addition to any diet, particularly for those needing a nutritious energy lift during a busy day.

Low-Calorie Options

Cucumber and Hummus Dip

Ingredients:

- 1 cucumber
- 1/4 cup hummus

Instructions:

1. Wash the cucumber thoroughly under running water.
2. Cut the cucumber into thin slices suitable for dipping.
3. Place the sliced cucumber on a plate with a small bowl of hummus.
4. Enjoy the cucumber slices by dipping them into the hummus.

Health Benefits:

- Cucumbers contain a high water content which helps in keeping you hydrated while being low in calories. They are also satisfying, helping to curb hunger pangs without weight gain.
- Hummus is a nutritious dip that combines protein and fiber, promoting a feeling of fullness and aiding in weight management.

Apple Slices with Almond Butter

Ingredients:

- 1 apple
- 2 tablespoons almond butter

Instructions:

1. Core and slice the apple into even sections.
2. Spread almond butter generously over each apple slice.

Health Benefits:

1. Apples are a great source of fiber and water, which help in managing hunger and maintaining low calorie intake. They also provide a natural sweetness.
2. Almond butter enhances this snack with its protein content and healthy fats, making it a balanced, nutritious choice that supports satiety and health.

Air-Popped Popcorn

Ingredients:

- 1/4 cup popcorn kernels
- A pinch of salt

Instructions:

1. Use a popcorn maker or a covered pan to air-pop the popcorn kernels. If using a pan, heat it over medium heat and shake occasionally until popping slows.
2. Once the popcorn is popped, immediately sprinkle it with a pinch of salt to enhance the flavor.

Health Benefits:

- Popcorn is a beneficial whole grain that is high in fiber, aiding in digestion and contributing to prolonged satiety.
- By air-popping the popcorn without oil, you keep the snack low in calories while still enjoying a crisp, satisfying treat.

Carrot Sticks with Cottage Cheese Dip

Ingredients:

- 1 cup carrots, sliced into sticks
- 1/2 cup low-fat cottage cheese
- Pinch of salt
- Pinch of pepper

Instructions:

1. In a small bowl, combine the low-fat cottage cheese with a pinch of salt and pepper until well mixed.
2. Serve the mixture as a dip with the carrot sticks.

Health Benefits:

- Carrots are an excellent source of beta-carotene and fiber, which contribute to their status as a nutritious, low-calorie snack option.
- Cottage cheese is a good source of protein and low in fat, enhancing this snack's ability to satisfy hunger efficiently while keeping calorie intake minimal.

Beverages

For those practicing intermittent fasting, the choice of beverages is particularly crucial. Liquids are often consumed not only during eating windows but also in fasting periods to help maintain hydration, alleviate hunger, and support metabolic health. Understanding which beverages are fasting-approved and exploring the variety of herbal teas and infusions can enhance the fasting experience while providing health benefits.

Fasting-Approved Drinks

1. Water:

Pure water is the cornerstone of hydration and is crucial for maintaining the body's functions. It does not break a fast and can be consumed in any amount.

Infused water: Enhance the flavour of plain water by infusing it with slices of fruits such as lemons, limes, and oranges or with herbs like mint or cucumber. These infusions add minimal to no calories and can make staying hydrated during fasting periods more enjoyable.

2. Black Coffee

Plain black coffee is another excellent choice during fasting periods. It contains almost no calories and can help suppress appetite. Additionally, coffee is rich in antioxidants and has been shown to support metabolic health.

Avoid adding sugar or milk, as these will increase the caloric content of the coffee, potentially breaking the fast.

3. Green Tea

Green tea is ideal for fasting due to its health benefits and low-calorie content. It contains catechins, powerful antioxidants that can help enhance metabolic rate and aid in weight loss.

Drink plain: Avoid adding sweeteners or milk to keep it fasting-approved.

4. Apple Cider Vinegar (ACV)

Diluted ACV: Mix one to two tablespoons of apple cider vinegar in a glass of water. This can aid digestion and stabilize blood sugar levels, which might spike after refeeding.

Consumption tip: Only consume diluted ACV to protect your teeth from acidity and to ensure it is gentle on your stomach.

Herbal Teas and Infusions

1. Peppermint Tea:

Benefits: Peppermint tea is excellent for digestion and can help relieve symptoms of bloating and indigestion. The refreshing flavour is also a natural stimulant and can provide a mental lift without caffeine jitters.

Brewing: Use fresh or dried peppermint leaves and steep in boiling water for 5-7 minutes, depending on desired strength.

2. Chamomile Tea:

Benefits: Chamomile is renowned for its calming properties, making it an excellent choice for drinking before bedtime, especially while fasting. It can help improve sleep quality and reduce stress.

Brewing: Steep chamomile flowers in hot water for about 5 minutes for a soothing tea.

3. Hibiscus Tea:

Benefits: Hibiscus tea can help lower blood pressure and is also high in Vitamin C, supporting immune health. Its tart flavor can be a pleasant refreshment during fasting windows.

Brewing: Use dried hibiscus flowers and steep in boiling water for 5 minutes. This tea can be enjoyed hot or iced.

4. Ginger Tea:

Benefits: Ginger tea is beneficial for digestive health and can help alleviate nausea and inflammation. It's also a great warm drink to stimulate your metabolism.

Brewing: Slice fresh ginger root and steep in boiling water for at least 10 minutes. Add lemon or a small amount of honey, if not fasting, for flavour enhancement.

5. Rooibos Tea:

Benefits: Rooibos is naturally caffeine-free and contains antioxidants that help protect the cells from oxidative stress. It's also believed to support bone health.

Brewing: Steep rooibos leaves in hot water for 5-7 minutes. This tea has a naturally sweet taste and a rich red color.

The selection of beverages during intermittent fasting is not merely about what is permissible but also what enhances the fasting experience both functionally and enjoyably. By choosing drinks that support hydration, metabolism, and overall health without breaking a fast, individuals can significantly enhance the effectiveness and sustainability of their fasting regimen. Herbal teas and other fasting-approved drinks are excellent tools in this journey, offering variety and health benefits while adhering to the fasting protocols.

CHAPTER 6

RECIPE - LUNCHES AND DINNERS

When following an intermittent fasting schedule, planning lunches and dinners that are nutritious, satisfying, and convenient can significantly enhance the diet's effectiveness. Proper meal planning helps maintain a balanced diet, manage portions, and minimize the time spent preparing meals each day. Below, we discuss strategies for meal-prepping success and provide essential tips for storing food to preserve freshness.

Meal Planning Strategies

Successful meal preparation begins with a well-thought-out plan. Here's how to ensure that lunches and dinners align with intermittent fasting goals and lifestyle:

Plan Your Menu Weekly: Before the week begins, take some time to plan out your lunch and dinner menus. Consider the macronutrient balance—incorporate a good mix of protein, fats, and carbohydrates into each meal. This not only helps in shopping and preparation but also ensures variety and nutritional balance.

Batch Cooking: One of the most efficient strategies for meal preparation is batch cooking. This involves cooking large quantities of a few dishes that can be mixed and matched throughout the week. For instance, bake a large tray of chicken breasts, cook a big pot of quinoa or rice, and roast various vegetables. These can then be combined in different ways to create diverse meals throughout the week.

Use Themed Nights: To keep meal planning simple and fun, you can assign theme nights for each day of the week, such as Meatless Monday, Taco Tuesday, or Fish Friday. This method simplifies decision-making and grocery shopping, and the predictable pattern can make cooking less of a chore.

Incorporate Leftovers: Plan dinners that easily convert into lunches for the next day. This not only saves time but also reduces waste. Dishes like stews, casseroles, and roasts typically make excellent next-day meals.

Storage and Freshness Tips

Proper storage is key to maintaining the freshness and nutritional value of cooked foods. Here are some tips to ensure that your meals remain delicious and safe to eat:

Cool Down Quickly: To minimize the risk of bacterial growth, cool cooked foods rapidly before refrigeration. Spread them out on a wide surface or divide them into smaller containers that allow quicker cooling.

Use Airtight Containers: Store your meals in airtight containers to preserve freshness and prevent contamination. Transparent containers can be particularly useful as they allow you to see what's inside without opening them, reducing exposure to air.

Label Everything: Label your containers with the date of cooking and their contents. This not only helps organize the meals but also ensures that you use the oldest meals first, thereby reducing spoilage.

Freeze for Longevity: If you prepare meals that won't be consumed within a few days, freezing is an excellent option. Most cooked dishes, such as soups, stews, and baked dishes, can be frozen for several weeks. Just be sure to leave some space in the container, as liquids expand when frozen.

Refrigerator Organization: Keep your refrigerator organized to ensure good air circulation and maintain an optimal temperature of 37°F (3°C). Store ready-to-eat foods on top and raw ingredients below to prevent cross-contamination.

Regularly Check Inventory: Regularly check what you have in the fridge and pantry to use items that are close to expiration. This reduces waste and helps you plan meals around ingredients that need to be used up.

By following these meal planning and storage tips, you can simplify your food preparation process, enhance meal variety, and ensure that you have healthy, homemade meals ready to go. This supports your intermittent fasting regimen by making it easier to stick to healthy eating habits, ultimately contributing to better health outcomes and a more enjoyable dieting experience.

Vegetarian Lunch Recipes

Creating satisfying and nutritious vegetarian lunches involves a mix of creativity and strategic planning. Vegetarian diets can offer all the necessary macronutrients and micronutrients required for health, provided meals are well-composed. Here, we explore recipes for hearty salads and warm, comforting soups that are perfect for a vegetarian lunch, providing both nourishment and pleasure.

Salads That Satisfy

Quinoa and Black Bean Salad

Ingredients:

- 1 cup quinoa
- 2 cups water
- 1 can of black beans, drained and rinsed
- 1 red of bell pepper, diced
- 1 cup corn kernels (fresh or frozen)
- 1 small red onion, finely chopped
- 1/4 cup chopped cilantro
- Juice of 2 limes
- 1/4 cup olive oil
- One teaspoon cumin
- Add Salt and pepper to taste
- Avocado slices for topping

Method:

1. Rinse quinoa under cold water until water runs clear. Bring quinoa and water to a boil in a saucepan. Reduce heat to low, cover, and simmer until quinoa is tender and water is absorbed, about 15 minutes.
2. Put the cooked quinoa, black beans, corn, onion, cilantro, and bell pepper in a big bowl.
3. Mix the lime juice, olive oil, cumin, salt, and pepper in a small bowl. Drizzle the quinoa mixture on top, then toss to coat.
4. Assist the salad topped with avocado slices.

Benefits:

This salad is rich in protein from the quinoa and black beans, fiber, and healthy fats from olive oil and avocado. It's a comprehensive meal that supports energy levels and digestion, perfect for a filling lunch.

Roasted Sweet Potato and Kale Salad

Ingredients

- 2 large sweet potatoes, peeled and cubed
- 1 tablespoon olive oil
- 1 teaspoon smoked paprika
- Add Salt and pepper to taste
- 4 cups chopped kale
- 1/4 cup toasted pumpkin seeds
- 1/4 cup dried cranberries
- 2 ounces' goat cheese, crumbled
- For dressing:
- 3 tablespoons apple cider vinegar
- 1 tablespoon Dijon mustard
- 1 tablespoon honey
- 1/3 cup olive oil
- Salt and pepper to taste

Method:

1. Turn the oven on to 400°F, or 200°C. Add salt, pepper, paprika, and olive oil to sweet potatoes and toss. Place on a baking pan, then roast until soft, 20 to 25 minutes.
2. Place kale in a large bowl, and when sweet potatoes are done, add them to the kale while still hot (this helps soften the kale).
3. Add pumpkin seeds, cranberries, and goat cheese to the bowl.
4. For the dressing, whisk together vinegar, mustard, honey, and olive oil in a small bowl. Season with salt and pepper.
5. Drizzle the salad with the dressing and toss to mix. Assist
6. warm or at room temperature.

Benefits:

Kale and sweet potatoes provide a high fibre content that promotes satiety and aids digestion. Pumpkin seeds offer a crunch with zinc and magnesium, while goat cheese adds a creamy texture and additional protein.

Warm, Comforting Soups recipes

Tomato Basil Soup

Ingredients:

- 2 tablespoons olive oil
- 1 onion, chopped
- 3 cloves garlic, minced
- 1 can (28 ounces) whole tomatoes
- 2 cups vegetable broth
- 1/2 cup chopped fresh basil
- 1/2 cup heavy cream or coconut milk

- Salt and pepper to taste

Method

- In a big pot, warm up the olive oil over medium heat. Add the garlic and onion; sauté until onion is translucent.
- Add the veggie broth and tomatoes. Bring to a boil, then simmer for 20 minutes on low heat.

- Add basil and use an immersion blender to puree the soup until smooth.
- Stir in cream or coconut milk, and Add pepper and salt for seasoning.
- Heat through.
- Assist hot, garnished with additional basil if desired.

Benefits:

This soup is rich in vitamins A and C from tomatoes, which are antioxidants that support immune health. The addition of fresh basil enhances flavour and provides additional nutrients, while olive oil contributes healthy fats.

Lentil and Vegetable Soup

Ingredients

- 1 tablespoon olive oil
- 1 onion, diced

- 2 carrots, peeled and diced
- 2 celery
- stalks, diced
- 3 cloves garlic, minced
- 1 teaspoon ground cumin
- 1/2 teaspoon ground coriander
- 1 cup dried lentils, rinsed
- 1 bay leaf
- 6 cups vegetable broth
- 2 cups chopped kale
- Salt and pepper to taste

Method:

1. Warm up the olive oil in a large pot over medium heat. Add onion, carrots, celery, and garlic. Cook until vegetables are softened.
2. Stir in cumin Add cilantro, then heat for a minute until fragrant.
3. Include lentils, bay leaf, and vegetable broth. Heat up to a boil, after which lower the heat and simmer the lentils, uncovered, for about 25 minutes, or until they are soft.
4. Add kale in the last 5 minutes of cooking. Season with salt and pepper.
5. Remove bay leaf before serving.

Benefits

Plant-based sources of fiber and protein include lentils.

This soup is hearty and satisfying while providing a rich array of minerals and vitamins from the added vegetables.

These vegetarian lunch recipes not only satisfy taste buds but also nourish the body with essential nutrients needed for energy and health, making them perfect for anyone following a vegetarian diet or looking for healthy meal options.

Non-Vegetarian Lunch Recipes

Non-vegetarian lunches offer a rich source of high-quality protein and essential nutrients that are crucial for maintaining muscle mass, supporting cellular functions, and ensuring overall health. Incorporating fish, poultry, and meat into meals can provide these benefits, especially when meals are crafted following the balanced plate principles. Here, we explore nutritious and satisfying non-vegetarian lunch recipes that align with these guidelines.

Fish, Poultry, and Meat Dishes

Grilled Salmon with Quinoa Salad

Ingredient

- 4 salmon fillets (4 oz each)
- 1 tablespoon olive oil
- 1 teaspoon lemon zest
- 2 tablespoons lemon juice
- 1 cup quinoa
- 2 cups water
- 1/2 cup halvedcherry tomatoes

- cucumber, diced1/2
- 1/4 cup red onion, finely chopped
- 1/4 cup feta cheese, crumbled
- 2 tablespoons fresh parsley, chopped
- Add Salt and pepper to taste

Method

1. Rinse quinoa under cold water, then cook in boiling water until fluffy, about 15 minutes; set aside to cool.
2. Set the grill's temperature to medium-high. Salmon fillets should be rubbed with olive oil, salt, pepper, and lemon zest.
3. Fish should be cooked thoroughly after grilling for 4–5 minutes on each side.
4. Combine quinoa, tomatoes, cucumber, onion, feta, and parsley. Dress with lemon juice and olive oil, and Add pepper and salt for seasoning.
5. Serve grilled salmon on top of the quinoa salad.

Benefits

Salmon is rich in omega-3 fatty acids, which is excellent for heart and brain health. Quinoa is a gluten-free source of protein and fibre that helps stabilize blood sugar levels, while vegetables and feta add freshness, flavour, and additional nutrients.

Chicken Avocado Wrap

Ingredients

- 2 cups cooked chicken breast, shredded
- 2 large whole wheat wraps
- 1 ripe avocado, mashed
- 1 small red bell pepper, sliced
- 1/2 cup spinach leaves

- 1/4 cup Greek yogurt
- 2 tablespoons cilantro, chopped
- Juice of 1 lime
- Add Salt and pepper to taste

Method:

1. Lay out the wraps and spread mashed avocado over the surfaces.
2. Top with chicken, bell pepper slices, and spinach.
3. In a small bowl, mix Greek yoghurt with lime juice, cilantro, salt, and pepper. Drizzle over the fillings.
4. Roll up the wraps tightly, slice in half, and serve.

Benefits

This wrap is a balanced meal containing protein from the chicken, healthy fats from the avocado, and complex carbs from the whole wheat wrap. The Greek yoghurt adds a creamy texture and probiotics.

Beef Stir-Fry with Mixed Vegetables:

Ingredients

- 1 lb lean beef strips
- 2 tablespoons soy sauce
- 1 tablespoon sesame oil
- 1 garlic clove, minced
- 1 inch ginger, minced

- 2 cups broccoli florets
- 1 red bell pepper, julienned
- 1 carrot, julienned
- 1/2 cup snap peas
- 1 onion, sliced
- Sesame seeds for garnish

Method

1. Sesame oil should be heated over medium-high heat in a big pan or wok. Add the ginger and garlic, and briefly sauté.
2. Add beef strips and soy sauce, stir-frying until the beef is just cooked.
3. Add broccoli, bell pepper, carrot, snap peas, and onion. Continue to stir-fry until vegetables are tender-crisp.
4. Sprinkle with sesame seeds before serving.

Benefits

Beef is a good source of iron and protein, which are vital for energy and muscle maintenance. The colourful vegetables provide vitamins and antioxidants, which help combat oxidative stress and inflammation.

Balanced Plate Principles

The concept of a "balanced plate" is vital for meal planning, especially when incorporating meat, which should not overwhelm the dish but rather be part of a holistic meal:

Half of the Plate: Vegetables

Aim to fill at least half of your plate with vegetables. This ensures a high intake of fibre, vitamins, and minerals, which helps with digestion and provides essential nutrients.

One-Quarter of the Plate Proteins

One-quarter of the plate should consist of lean proteins such as chicken, fish, or beef. This proportion supports muscle repair and growth without excessive calorie intake

One-Quarter of the Plate: Whole Grains or Starchy Vegetables

The remaining quarter should include whole grains like quinoa, brown rice, or starchy vegetables such as sweet potatoes. These complex carbohydrates provide sustained energy and are essential for overall health.

Add Healthy Fats

Incorporate healthy fats such as olive oil, avocados, or nuts. These are essential for hormonal balance, brain function, and cell integrity.

These non-vegetarian lunch recipes adhere to the balanced plate principles and ensure that meals are nutritious, satisfying, and supportive of a healthy lifestyle. They are ideal for those following intermittent fasting schedules, providing the necessary energy and nutrients for the rest of the day.

Vegetarian Dinner Recipes

Creating vegetarian dinners that are both light and fulfilling can be a rewarding approach to maintaining a balanced diet, particularly for those practising intermittent fasting. These meals can deliver essential nutrients without the heaviness associated with meat dishes, making them ideal for evening meals that complement a fasting regimen.

Light Yet Filling Options

Stuffed Bell Peppers

Ingredients

- 4 large bell peppers, tops cut away and seeds removed
- 1 cup cooked brown rice
- 1 can black beans, rinsed and drained
- 1 cup corn kernels (fresh or frozen)
- 1/2 cup chopped tomatoes
- 1/2 cup grated Monterey Jack cheese
- 1/4 cup finely chopped cilantro
- 1 teaspoon cumin
- Salt and pepper to taste
- Sour cream for serving (optional)

Method:

1. Preheat 190°C or 375°F in the oven.
2. In bowl mix brown rice, black beans, corn, tomatoes, half of the cheese, cilantro, cumin, salt, and pepper.
3. After hollowing out the bell peppers, evenly stuff the insides and put them in a baking tray.

4. Top with the remaining cheese and cover with aluminium foil.
5. Bake in the preheated oven for about 30 minutes, then remove the foil and continue baking until the peppers are tender and the cheese is bubbly about 15 more minutes.
6. Serve hot, topped with a dollop of sour cream if desired.

Benefits

This dish is not only visually appealing but also packed with fiber from beans and brown rice, which promotes satiety. The cheese provides calcium and protein, making the meal balanced and satisfying.

Zucchini and Tomato Tart with Feta

Ingredients:

- 1 sheet puff pastry, thawed
- 2 medium zucchinis, thinly sliced
- 2 tomatoes, thinly sliced
- 1/2 cup crumbled feta cheese
- 2 tablespoons fresh basil, chopped
- 1 tablespoon olive oil
- Salt and pepper to taste

Method

1. Turn the oven on to 400°F, or 200°C.

2. Roll out the puff pastry on a parchment paper-lined baking sheet.
3. Arrange zucchini and tomato slices on the pastry, overlapping slightly. Sprinkle with salt, pepper, and olive oil.
4. Bake for 25 minutes, then sprinkle feta cheese and basil over the top.
5. Bake for another 5-10 minutes or until the pastry is golden and veggies are tender.
6. Serve warm.

Benefit

Zucchini and tomatoes are low in calories but high in vitamins and water, making them perfect for a light dinner. The feta adds a tangy flavor and boosts the protein content.

Quick Fixes for Busy Nights

Lemon Garlic Pasta with Asparagus

Ingredients

- 8 oz pasta (such as spaghetti or fettuccine)
- 1 bunch asparagus, trimmed and cut into 1-inch pieces
- 3 tablespoons olive oil
- 3 cloves garlic, minced
- Zest and juice of 1 lemon
- 1/4 cup grated Parmesan cheese
- Add Salt and pepper to taste
- Red pepper flakes (optional)

Method

1. Bring a large pot of salted water to a boil. Add pasta and cook according to package instructions. In the last 3 minutes of cooking, add asparagus.
2. Drain pasta and asparagus, reserving 1/2 cup of the pasta water.
3. In the same saucepan, warm the olive oil over medium heat. Add the garlic and heat for one minute, or until fragrant.
4. Add the pasta, asparagus, lemon zest, and lemon juice back to the pot. Toss to combine, adding reserved pasta water a little at a time until the sauce coats the pasta lightly.
5. Add the Parmesan cheese and season with pepper, salt, and, if desired, red pepper flakes.
6. Serve immediately.

Benefits

This dish is quick to prepare, taking about 20 minutes' total, but doesn't skimp on nutrition. Asparagus is rich in folate and vitamins A, C, and K, while the lemon boosts the vitamin C content and adds a fresh flavor.

Quick Chickpea Curry

Ingredients

- 1 tablespoon coconut oil
- 1 onion, chopped
- 2 cloves garlic, minced
- 1 tablespoon grated ginger
- 1 tablespoon curry powder
- 1 can (14 oz) diced tomatoes
- 1 can (14 oz)
- chickpeas, drained and rinsed
- 1 can (14 oz) coconut milk
- Salt and pepper to taste
- Fresh cilantro for garnish

Method

1. In a large skillet set over medium heat, warm the coconut oil. When the onion becomes transparent, add the ginger, garlic, and onion and sauté.
2. Stir in curry powder and cook for another minute.
3. Add tomatoes, chickpeas, and coconut milk. Bring to a simmer and cook for 10-15 minutes or until slightly thickened.
4. Season with salt and pepper. Garnish with cilantro before serving.

Benefits

Chickpeas provide a hearty dose of protein and fibre, making this curry filling nutritious. Coconut milk adds richness and healthy fats, while the spices contribute antioxidants and anti-inflammatory benefits.

These vegetarian dinner recipes are designed to be both fulfilling and quick to prepare, perfect for evenings when time is short but a nutritious meal is still a priority. Whether looking for a light meal or something to satiate hunger without being overly heavy, these recipes provide delicious and healthy options.

Non-Vegetarian Dinner Recipes

Non-vegetarian dinners, when done right, can provide a rich source of essential proteins, vitamins, and minerals that help repair the body, support muscle growth, and ensure overall health. Creating nutrient-dense meals that are flavorful and satisfying is key, especially for those incorporating them into an intermittent fasting regimen. Here, we discuss recipes that not only end the day on a nutritious note but also utilize cooking techniques that maximize flavor retention.

Nutrient-Dense Meals to End the Day

Herb-Roasted Chicken with Root Vegetables

Ingredients

- 4 chicken thighs, bone-in and skin-on
- 2 carrots, peeled and chopped
- 2 parsnips, peeled and chopped
- 1 sweet potato, peeled and cubed
- 1 onion, quartered
- 3 cloves garlic, minced
- 2 tablespoons olive oil
- 1 teaspoon dried rosemary
- 1 teaspoon dried thyme
- Add Salt and pepper to taste

Method

1. Turn on oven to 375°F (190°C).
2. Combine the sweet potato, onion, parsnips, rosemary, thyme, olive oil, and salt & pepper in a big bowl.
3. Spread the vegetables in a single layer on a large baking sheet.
4. Top the veggies with the chicken thighs. Season chicken with salt and pepper and a bit more olive oil.
5. Roast in the preheated oven for about 45-50 Bake for 50 minutes, or until the veggies are soft and the chicken is cooked through and golden.
6. Warm up and serve..

Benefits

This meal is packed with high-quality protein from the chicken, while the root vegetables provide a good source of beta-carotene, vitamin C, potassium, and fibre. The herbs and roasting process enhance the natural flavours of the ingredients without needing excess salt or fat.

Pan-Seared Salmon with Garlic Spinach:

Ingredients

- 4 salmon fillets, skin-on
- 2 tablespoons olive oil
- 4 cups fresh spinach
- 2 cloves garlic, minced
- Lemon wedges for serving
- Salt and black pepper to taste

Method

1. In a nonstick skillet, heat one tablespoon of olive oil over medium-high heat.
2. Season the salmon with salt and pepper, and place it skin-side down in the skillet. Cook for 6-7 minutes on each side or until the skin is crispy and the salmon is cooked through.

3. Remove salmon and place aside. Add to the same skillet another tablespoon of olive oil and sauté garlic until fragrant.
4. Add spinach and sauté until wilted, seasoning with salt and pepper.
5. Serve the salmon with sautéed spinach and a squeeze of fresh lemon juice.

Benefits

Salmon is an excellenta supply of fatty acids omega-3 , which is crucial for cardiovascular health and cognitive functions. Spinach provides iron and folate, which are important for blood health and DNA synthesis.

Cooking Techniques That Retain Flavor

Moist Heat Cooking

Techniques such as poaching or steaming are excellent for cooking delicate proteins like fish. These methods use gentle heat and moisture for cooking the food, preserving its moisture, texture, and nutrients while enhancing its natural flavors.

Roasting

Roasting uses dry heat to cook the food evenly while caramelizing the natural sugars in vegetables and browning the meat. This technique not only enhances the taste but also preserves the nutrients and flavors of the ingredients.

Searing

Searing meat quickly on high heat locks in flavors and juices, creating a tasty crust. It's particularly effective for steaks and fillets, providing a textural contrast between the exterior and the moist interior.

Slow Cooking

Slow cooking is ideal for tougher cuts of meat. The long, low-temperature cooking process breaks down collagen in meat, making it tender and flavorful while allowing herbs and seasonings to infuse deeply.

Use of Herbs and Spices

Instead of relying heavily on salt, using a variety of herbs and spices can significantly enhance the natural flavours of meats and vegetables. Fresh herbs, robust spices, and aromatic seasonings not only add depth to the dishes but also contribute additional health benefits.

By incorporating these cooking techniques and focusing on nutrient-dense ingredients, non-vegetarian dinners can be both a delightful and healthful way to end the day. These meals support a balanced diet, cater to those on intermittent fasting plans, and ensure that diners enjoy a satisfying and flavorful culinary experience.

CHAPTER 7

OVERCOMING CHALLENGES AND PLATEAUS

Adopting intermittent fasting as a lifestyle choice brings many health benefits, such as improved metabolic health, increased fat loss, and enhanced longevity. However, the journey is full of challenges. Individuals often face hurdles such as hunger pangs and navigating social and family meals, which can make adherence difficult. Additionally, plateaus in weight loss or health improvements can demotivate even the most disciplined practitioners. Understanding how to overcome these obstacles effectively is crucial for long-term success and sustained health benefits.

Managing Hunger Pangs

One of the most immediate and difficult challenges for those new to intermittent fasting is dealing with hunger pangs. These intense cravings can test the willpower of even seasoned fasters. The key to managing these uncomfortable sensations lies in strategic meal planning and hydration. Drinking ample fluids, particularly water and herbal teas, can help fill the stomach and reduce the perception of hunger. Additionally, planning nutrient-dense meals that are rich in fiber and protein during eating windows can prolong feelings of satiety. Foods like vegetables, legumes, whole grains, lean meats, and eggs are excellent for keeping hunger at bay.

Engaging in activities that distract from thoughts of eating can also be beneficial. Whether it's a hobby, exercise, or meditation, keeping the mind occupied can prevent it from fixating on food and help one adhere to fasting periods without succumbing to cravings.

Navigating Social and Family Meals

Social gatherings and family meals are significant aspects of life but can pose challenges to maintaining an intermittent fasting schedule. The social pressure to eat outside fasting windows can be particularly challenging during holidays, celebrations, or even casual get-togethers. To handle these situations, it's advisable to plan by adjusting fasting periods to accommodate important social meals. Flexibility is key in intermittent fasting; adjusting fasting windows by a few hours to share a meal with loved ones can make the diet more practical and socially enjoyable.

Communicating openly with friends and family about one's fasting regimen can also alleviate some of the social pressures. Most people are supportive once they understand the health reasons behind intermittent fasting. In instances where adjusting fasting times isn't possible, choosing lighter meals or smaller portions can help mitigate some of the impact on the fasting schedule.

Overcoming Plateaus

Many individuals eventually encounter a plateau in their weight loss or health gains, a common aspect of any long-term dietary plan. Overcoming a plateau requires revisiting and revising one's fasting and dietary strategies. Strategies such as altering the fasting window (e.g., shifting from a 16:8 to an 18:6 schedule), introducing caloric variability, and increasing physical activity can help reinvigorate the body's response to fasting.

Varying the types of foods consumed during eating windows and ensuring a balanced intake of macronutrients can also prevent the body from adapting too comfortably to a set routine. Incorporating different types of exercise or increasing the intensity can further enhance metabolic rate and break through weight loss plateaus.

Practical Tips for Sustained Success

1. **Stay Hydrated:** Drink plenty of water throughout the day to help manage hunger and maintain metabolic health.

2. **Be Flexible**: Adjust fasting periods to better fit social occasions and lifestyle demands.

3. **Mix Up Your Routine:** Change your fasting schedule and workout regimen to keep your metabolic rate high.

4. **Monitor Your Intake:** Use food tracking apps to accurately measure your caloric intake during eating windows.

5. **Seek Social Support:** Communicate with family and friends about your fasting regime to garner support and understanding.

6. **Reflect and Adapt:** Regularly assess your progress and be willing to make dietary and lifestyle adjustments as needed.

By addressing these common challenges with thoughtful strategies and a flexible approach, individuals practicing intermittent fasting can enhance their ability to maintain this healthful eating pattern over the long term. This not only helps in achieving desired weight loss and health goals but also in integrating intermittent fasting into a sustainable lifestyle.

Dealing with Weight Plateaus

Intermittent fasting has been lauded for its ability to facilitate weight loss and improve metabolic health. However, many practitioners encounter a common hurdle known as the weight plateau, where initial rapid weight loss slows down or completely stalls. Understanding why weight plateaus happen and learning strategies to overcome them is crucial for those looking to achieve long-term success with intermittent fasting.

Understanding Weight Plateaus

Weight plateaus occur when the body adapts to the dietary and energy expenditure changes brought about by any new diet or exercise regimen. Initially, significant weight loss can be seen, primarily due to the loss of water weight and some fat mass. However, as the body adapts to reduced calorie intake and changes in metabolic demands, the rate of weight loss can decrease, leading to a plateau.

Several factors contribute to this phenomenon:

Metabolic Adaptation: The human body is incredibly adept at surviving caloric deficits. When you consistently consume fewer calories, the body compensates by lowering its metabolic rate to conserve energy. This adaptive response can significantly slow down weight loss.

Loss of Muscle Mass: Often, weight loss involves losing both fat and muscle, especially if the diet does not contain adequate protein or if physical activity is lacking. Since muscle tissue burns more calories than fat tissue, its reduction can further decrease the metabolic rate.

Decreased Caloric Deficit: As a person loses weight, their energy requirement decreases. A smaller body expends fewer calories during daily activities and at rest. Thus, the initial caloric intake that led to weight loss may no longer suffice to create a large enough deficit, contributing to a plateau.

Strategies to Break Through Weight Plateaus

Breaking through a weight plateau involves adjusting dietary intake, fasting protocols, and physical activity levels to reinitiate weight loss. Here are several effective strategies:

Reassess Caloric Needs: As body weight decreases, so do caloric requirements. Recalculate your basal metabolic rate (BMR) based on your new weight to understand how many calories your body needs daily and adjust your eating plans accordingly.

Incorporate Exercise: Increasing physical activity can boost metabolic rate and help overcome a plateau. Focus on strength training exercises to build muscle mass, which can increase your resting metabolic rate and aid in more effective calorie burn.

Vary Fasting Windows: Altering your intermittent fasting schedule can also help break a plateau. If you typically follow a 16:8 fasting regimen, try switching to a 20:4 format a few days a week or experiment with full 24-hour fasts. This variation can challenge the body and increase fat metabolism.

Change Macronutrient Ratios: Adjusting the proportions of carbohydrates, fats, and proteins in your diet can have a significant impact. Increasing protein intake can enhance satiety and reduce overall caloric intake while adjusting carb and fat intake can help manage insulin levels and support fat burning.

Implement Caloric Cycling: Also known as calorie shifting, this strategy involves varying your calorie intake on a daily or weekly basis. By having higher-calorie days and lower-calorie days, you can prevent a slowdown in metabolic rate that typically accompanies a consistent caloric deficit.

Enhance Sleep Quality: Poor-quality sleep can affect several metabolic processes, including insulin sensitivity and hunger hormones like ghrelin and leptin. Improving sleep quality can enhance weight loss efforts and help break through plateaus.

Stay Hydrated: Increased water intake can boost metabolism, suppress appetite, and reduce overall calorie intake, aiding in weight loss continuation.

By understanding the physiological underpinnings of weight plateaus and employing strategic methods to modify their diet and lifestyle, individuals can continue to make progress in their weight loss journeys. The key to overcoming plateaus is flexibility—being willing to adapt your approach in response to changes in your body and its needs. This adaptability not only helps in advancing towards weight goals but also supports overall health and well-being in the long-term practice of intermittent fasting.

Emotional and Psychological Aspects

Intermittent fasting, while beneficial for physical health with its potential for weight loss and metabolic enhancements, also involves significant emotional and psychological challenges. These aspects are crucial as they profoundly affect the sustainability and overall effectiveness of the fasting regimen. Addressing mood swings and the importance of robust support systems for maintaining motivation are essential components discussed in this chapter.

Managing Mood Swings

Mood swings during intermittent fasting can stem from several sources, primarily hormonal fluctuations and changes in blood sugar levels, which can impact brain function and emotional stability. As the body adapts to a new eating schedule and shifts its energy source from glucose to fatty acids and ketone bodies, this transition can trigger irritability and anxiety due to increased cortisol levels. Understanding these causes is the first step in managing these mood fluctuations effectively.

To combat mood swings, incorporating a balanced diet during eating windows is crucial. A mix of proteins, healthy fats, and complex carbohydrates can stabilize blood sugar levels and enhance mood. Proteins and fats provide a more consistent energy source that does not spike blood glucose levels, thereby avoiding the crashes that lead to mood swings. Complex carbohydrates are important as well, as they can help increase serotonin production, a hormone that stabilizes our mood, feelings of well-being, and happiness.

Implementing a gradual approach to fasting can also ease the emotional and physiological impacts. Starting with shorter fasting periods and slowly extending the fasting window can help the body adjust more smoothly, reducing the severity of mood swings.

Incorporating mindfulness practices such as meditation and deep-breathing exercises can be highly beneficial in managing stress and enhancing emotional resilience. These techniques help in maintaining focus and calmness through the fasting process, mitigating feelings of anxiety and irritability.

Support Systems and Motivation

The role of a supportive environment and continuous motivation cannot be overstated in the context of intermittent fasting. Building a network of support through friends, family, or community groups who understand and respect one's fasting regimen can provide emotional comfort and practical advice.

Setting clear and achievable goals can also play a critical role in maintaining motivation. These objectives should focus not only on weight loss but also on other health metrics, such as improved energy levels, better sleep quality, or enhanced physical stamina.

Achieving these goals can provide a significant motivational boost and help sustain the fasting practice over the long term.

Maintaining motivation can also be bolstered by keeping a journal or log, where one can track not only dietary intake and fasting hours but also emotional health and physical changes. Documenting this journey can help identify patterns that affect mood and energy levels, making it easier to adjust practices to better meet personal health goals.

Lastly, seeking professional guidance from healthcare providers or dietitians who are knowledgeable about intermittent fasting can offer a motivational and instructional layer of support. They can provide tailored advice that aligns with individual health needs and lifestyle choices, ensuring both physical and psychological needs are met.

Managing the emotional and psychological aspects of intermittent fasting involves:

- Understanding the underlying causes of mood swings.
- Implementing strategic dietary adjustments.
- Leveraging both community support and professional guidance.

By addressing these areas, individuals can enhance their ability to maintain this healthful eating pattern and achieve their long-term health and wellness goals.

Adapting Fasting for Health Issues

Intermittent fasting has gained popularity as a flexible dietary approach with various health benefits, including improved metabolic profiles and reduced inflammation. However, individuals with chronic health conditions such as diabetes, thyroid disorders, and other metabolic diseases must approach fasting with caution.

Tailoring fasting protocols to accommodate these health issues while ensuring safety and efficacy requires a nuanced understanding and, often, the involvement of healthcare professionals.

Fasting with Diabetes

Diabetes, characterized by impaired insulin production and fluctuating blood glucose levels, poses significant challenges for those wishing to undertake fasting. Fasting can affect blood sugar levels dramatically, which is particularly concerning for people with diabetes who are dependent on insulin or other glucose-lowering medications.

Type 1 Diabetes: For individuals with type 1 diabetes, fasting without careful monitoring and medical guidance can lead to severe hypoglycemia or ketoacidosis. The lack of insulin production in type 1 diabetes means that adjusting insulin doses during fasting periods is critical and must be managed by a healthcare provider.

Type 2 Diabetes: Those with type 2 diabetes may find intermittent fasting beneficial as it can improve insulin sensitivity and help in weight management. However, medication types and timings may need to be adjusted to prevent hypoglycemia during fasting windows. Monitoring blood glucose levels is essential to avoid adverse effects.

For people with diabetes interested in fasting, starting with shorter fasting windows and gradually increasing the duration under medical supervision can help gauge individual tolerance. It's also crucial to maintain a diet rich in fiber, healthy fats, and proteins during eating windows to stabilize blood sugar levels.

Fasting with Thyroid Issues

Thyroid disorders, such as hypothyroidism and hyperthyroidism, affect metabolism significantly and can complicate the effects of intermittent fasting.

Hypothyroidism: Fasting might slow down metabolism further in those with an already underactive thyroid. This can exacerbate symptoms like fatigue, depression, and weight gain. Patients should approach fasting cautiously, as caloric restriction might impair thyroid hormone production.

Hyperthyroidism: For those with an overactive thyroid, fasting needs careful consideration as well. The increased metabolism might lead to more severe weight loss and muscle wasting. Balancing nutrient intake and possibly adjusting medication during fasting periods are necessary steps.

Individuals with thyroid issues should consult with an endocrinologist to discuss their plans to start fasting. Regular monitoring of thyroid function tests, alongside careful adjustment of thyroid medications, might be required.

Other Health Conditions

Intermittent fasting might affect or be affected by other health conditions, including but not limited to cardiovascular diseases, gastrointestinal disorders, or chronic kidney disease. Each condition may have specific implications that require adjustments to fasting plans.

Cardiovascular Diseases: Patients with heart conditions should ensure that fasting does not conflict with their cardiac medications and does not cause electrolyte imbalances that might affect heart rhythms.

Gastrointestinal Disorders: Conditions like gastritis or ulcers could worsen with prolonged stomach acidity during fasting. A modified fasting schedule or preventive medications might be necessary.

Chronic Kidney Disease: Fasting might alter fluid and electrolyte balance, which can be risky in kidney disease. Careful planning and avoiding prolonged fasts are crucial.

When to Consult a Healthcare Provider

Consulting with a healthcare provider is critical under the following circumstances:

Pre-existing Chronic Conditions: Anyone with chronic conditions like diabetes or thyroid disorders should consult their doctor before beginning intermittent fasting. This consultation should include a discussion about the potential risks and benefits, along with a plan for monitoring and adjusting therapy as needed.

Medication Adjustments: Changes to any medication regime, particularly for conditions like diabetes where dosing might need to match food intake, require professional oversight.

Symptoms During Fasting: If adverse symptoms such as severe fatigue, dizziness, confusion, or irregular heartbeats occur, it's imperative to seek medical advice. These could be signs of dangerous side effects like hypoglycemia or electrolyte imbalance.

Regular Monitoring: Ongoing monitoring of the condition with a healthcare provider can help in safely maintaining fasting routines. This might include regular blood tests or other diagnostic measures.

Intermittent fasting offers numerous health benefits, but it is not suitable for everyone, especially those with significant health issues.

Customizing fasting protocols to individual health needs with the guidance of a healthcare provider is essential for maintaining health and safety.

Fasting During Special Occasions

Adhering to an intermittent fasting schedule during holidays, vacations, and special occasions can be challenging. These events often disrupt daily routines and are centred around meals and festivities that can complicate strict fasting regimens. However, with thoughtful preparation and adaptive strategies, it is possible to maintain fasting practices without sacrificing the enjoyment of these special times.

Fasting During Holidays and Vacations

Holidays and vacations typically involve an abundance of food and altered daily schedules, which can make sticking to a regular fasting plan difficult. One effective method to manage this is by planning. Anticipate the event's meal schedule and adjust your fasting windows accordingly. For instance, if a large dinner is planned, you might choose to skip breakfast to accommodate a later eating window, thus aligning your fasting period with the day's activities.

Adopting a flexible fasting protocol during these periods can also alleviate the stress of strict adherence. Switching from a daily intermittent fasting approach to a more relaxed format, such as the 5:2 methods—eating normally for five days and restricting calories on two days—can provide the necessary flexibility. This method allows for adjustment based on social engagements and can be less intrusive to your holiday or vacation experience.

Mindfulness during meal times is another crucial strategy. Being mindful involves:

- Paying close attention to what and how much you eat.

- Recognizing when you are satiated rather than stuffed.
- Choosing foods that are both nourishing and enjoyable.

This practice helps maintain a balance between indulging in favorite foods and not overeating.

Increasing physical activity is another beneficial approach during breaks. Holidays often provide more free time; using this time to engage in physical activities such as walking, playing sports, or exploring new places can help offset additional calorie intake and contribute to overall energy balance and health.

Keeping on Track

Staying on course with intermittent fasting during special occasions requires realistic expectations and readiness to manage deviations from the norm. Clear communication of your fasting intentions with friends and family can enhance support from your social circle, making it easier to navigate communal eating situations.

Prioritizing quality over quantity is essential. Opt for dishes that are high in nutrients and will satisfy longer rather than empty calories that offer little satiety. This selective approach can significantly enhance meal satisfaction and support your fasting and health goals.

Setbacks may occur, and it's important to handle them with grace. If you find yourself eating outside your planned fasting window, avoid self-reproach. Instead, focus on resuming your fasting schedule as planned and learn from the experience to better prepare for future occasions.

Technological tools can also play a supportive role. Many apps are designed to track fasting periods, provide reminders, and offer motivational resources. These can be particularly useful during times when maintaining a fasting routine feels more challenging.

Fasting during holidays and vacations presents unique challenges, these can be effectively managed through planning, flexibility, mindful eating, and physical activity. By adapting your approach to fit the occasion and maintaining a focus on overall health and well-being, you can enjoy festive times without compromising your fasting regimen. This balanced approach not only preserves the physical benefits of intermittent fasting but also enhances the enjoyment and cultural richness of special occasions.

CHAPTER 8

ADVANCED FASTING TECHNIQUES

As practitioners become more accustomed to intermittent fasting, many look towards more advanced fasting methods to enhance their health benefits. Periodic prolonged fasting, which involves extending the fasting period significantly beyond the typical daily windows, is one such approach. This chapter explores the benefits of periodic prolonged fasting, outlines protocols to follow, and provides guidance on how to undertake these fasts safely.

Periodic Prolonged Fasting

Periodic prolonged fasting refers to fasting periods that typically last from 48 hours to several days. Unlike intermittent fasting, which is done daily, prolonged fasting is undertaken less frequently, perhaps once a month or quarterly, depending on individual health goals and tolerance.

Benefits of Periodic Prolonged Fasting:

The benefits of engaging in prolonged fasting are substantial and include enhanced cellular repair processes, improved metabolic health, and significant impacts on ageing and longevity. Here are some of the key benefits:

Autophagy: This process, where cells cleanse themselves of old and malfunctioning components, is significantly upregulated during extended fasts. Autophagy is linked to reduced inflammation, a lower risk of neurological diseases, and better cellular performance.

Hormonal Reset: Prolonged fasting can help reset various hormonal balances in the body. It improves insulin sensitivity, which can help manage or prevent type 2 diabetes. Hormones such as ghrelin (the hunger hormone) are modulated, which can help recalibrate appetite regulation.

Reduction in Inflammatory Markers: Extended fasts have been shown to decrease markers of inflammation, which is a root cause of many chronic diseases, including arthritis, heart disease, and stroke.

Psychological Resilience: The challenge of completing a prolonged fast can also enhance mental toughness and provide a sense of accomplishment that can be psychologically beneficial.

Protocols for Periodic Prolonged Fasting:

Engaging in prolonged fasting safely requires careful planning and consideration of one's physical and medical status:

Preparation Phase: Before embarking on a prolonged fast, it is advisable to reduce calorie intake over a few days gradually and to increase hydration. This can help ease the transition into the fast, making it less of a shock to the system.

During the Fast: Consume plenty of water throughout the fast. Salt (sodium), potassium, and magnesium supplements are vital for maintaining electrolyte balance, especially during longer fasts. It's critical to pay attention to your body during the fast. If symptoms such as severe dizziness, confusion, or extreme weakness occur, it's crucial to consider ending the fast.

Breaking the Fast: How you end your fast is as important as the fast itself. Break the fast gently with a small meal that is easy to digest—such as a soup or a smoothie—and gradually reintroduce more substantial foods over several days to avoid refeeding syndrome, a potentially fatal condition caused by the rapid reintroduction of food after a period of malnutrition.

How to Safely Undertake Periodic Prolonged Fasting

Safety should be the top priority when engaging in any form of prolonged fasting. Here are detailed steps to ensure a safe fasting experience:

Medical Consultation: Before starting a prolonged fast, especially for the first time, it is crucial to consult with a healthcare provider, particularly if you have underlying health conditions such as diabetes low blood pressure, or if you are on medications.

Monitor Your Body: Regular monitoring of vital signs like blood pressure and heart rate can be helpful, especially if you have been fasting for longer than 48 hours. Understanding the signs of when to stop fasting due to health concerns is vital.

Environment: Ensure you are in a supportive environment where you can rest and not exert yourself physically. The body's energy levels will be lower than usual, and significant physical exertion is not recommended.

Post-Fast Care: Plan for a recovery phase after the fast. Your digestive system will need time to adapt to regular food intake. Start with liquids, then soft foods, and gradually increase to solid foods, monitoring how your body responds.

Periodic prolonged fasting, when done correctly, can be a powerful tool to enhance health and longevity. However, it requires a well-considered approach and should always be tailored to individual health needs and life circumstances, ideally under professional guidance, to maximize benefits and minimize risks.

Autophagy and Its Benefits

Autophagy, derived from the Greek words for "self" and "eating," is a crucial biological process by which cells degrade and recycle their components. This process plays a vital role in cleaning out damaged cells, regenerating new cells, and maintaining proper cellular function. The relationship between autophagy and fasting is particularly significant, as fasting is known to enhance the autophagic process significantly. This chapter explores the intricate science of cellular cleansing through autophagy and details how fasting acts as a trigger for this beneficial cellular mechanism.

The Science of Cellular Cleansing

Autophagy is an essential cellular process that prevents cellular clutter by disposing of damaged and dysfunctional cellular components. It is crucial for cell health, survival, and function. Autophagy involves several steps. Cellular material is first sequestered in double-membraned vesicles known as auto phagosomes. These auto phagosomes then fuse with lysosomes to form autolysosomes, where the cellular material is degraded and recycled.

This process helps to manage stress at the cellular level by removing damaged organelles, misfolded proteins, and pathogens. It plays a significant role in managing infections and immune response, reducing inflammation, and adapting to nutrient stress. By clearing out the old, damaged cellular parts, autophagy promotes renewal and efficiency within cells, which is crucial for preventing diseases such as neurodegeneration, cancers, and infections.

How Fasting Triggers Autophagy

Fasting initiates autophagy by creating a nutrient-deprived environment that forces cells to seek internal energy sources. The shift in the metabolic state required during fasting imposes a form of stress on cells that autophagy helps to mitigate by breaking down non-essential components to reuse for maintenance and repair processes.

Hormonal Changes and Energy Stress: The decrease in insulin levels during fasting is a critical trigger for autophagy. Lower insulin levels reduce the activity of the motor pathway, an important inhibitor of autophagy. Simultaneously, fasting increases levels of glucagon, which activates protein degradation pathways necessary for initiating autophagy.

Protein Deprivation: Fasting reduces the intake and availability of amino acids, which are the building blocks of proteins. In response, cells activate autophagy to recycle existing proteins to meet their amino acid requirements, thus maintaining cellular function and survival.

Safely Enhancing Autophagy Through Fasting

While fasting is an effective method to enhance autophagy, it must be undertaken with care, especially for prolonged periods, to avoid negative health impacts.

Gradual Initiation and Adequate Hydration: It is crucial for individuals new to fasting to start with shorter periods and gradually increase the duration. This approach helps the body adapt to energy stress without severe metabolic shock. During fasting, maintaining hydration is essential, as it supports kidney function and the flushing out of cellular debris generated during autophagy.

Balanced Nutrient Intake: During non-fasting periods, it is important to consume a balanced diet rich in micronutrients and macronutrients. This replenishment supports the body's recovery from fasting and provides the necessary materials for effective autophagy during the next fasting cycle.

Monitoring and Adjustment: Monitoring one's physical response to fasting and autophagy is crucial, particularly during extended fasting periods. If any adverse symptoms occur, it is advisable to reassess the fasting regime with the guidance of a healthcare professional.

Consulting with Healthcare Providers: It is essential to speak with a healthcare provider before embarking on fasting plan that aims to activate autophagy, particularly for individuals with pre-existing health conditions or those on medication. This precaution ensures that fasting is beneficial and not detrimental to health.

Autophagy is a vital metabolic process that promotes cellular health and longevity. Fasting is a powerful way to stimulate this process, offering benefits that extend beyond simple weight management to include profound health improvements. However, like any powerful tool, fasting should be used wisely and with an understanding of the underlying biological processes it influences to maximize health benefits while minimizing risks.

Combining Fasting With Keto

The integration of intermittent fasting and the ketogenic diet represents a powerful synergistic approach to enhancing health. Both strategies independently have robust health advantages, such as reduced body weight and enhanced metabolic health, and cognitive enhancement. When combined, these effects can be amplified, offering transformative health benefits greater than those of either approach alone. This chapter delves into the synergistic effects of combining fasting with a ketogenic diet and offers practical guidelines for those looking to merge these dietary strategies effectively.

Synergistic Effects on Health

The ketogenic diet emphasizes very minimal carbohydrate intake, moderate protein, and substantial fat consumption.

To push the body into ketosis, a metabolic state where fat is burned for energy instead of carbohydrates. Intermittent fasting alternates between eating and fasting periods, enhancing hormone function to facilitate weight loss and health improvements. The combination of these diets accelerates entry into ketosis while deepening the state, potentially increasing fat loss and metabolic health benefits.

One of the key benefits of combining intermittent fasting with the ketogenic diet is the enhanced ability of the body to utilize fat as its primary energy source. This is due to the extended periods of low insulin levels during fasting, which complements the fat-centric energy utilization of the ketogenic diet. This dual approach not only speeds up the fat loss process but also stabilizes blood sugar levels, enhancing overall metabolic health.

The combination also improves metabolic flexibility, which is the body's ability to switch between burning carbs and fats for energy seamlessly. This flexibility is crucial for maintaining energy levels, reducing hunger pangs, and minimizing the common side effects associated with transitioning to a fat-based metabolism.

Both strategies independently increase the levels of autophagy, a cellular cleaning process that removes damaged cells and regenerates new ones. When combined, this effect is magnified, potentially offering profound anti-ageing benefits and reducing the risk of several chronic diseases by maintaining cellular health.

Guidelines for Combining Diets

Successfully combining intermittent fasting with the ketogenic diet requires careful consideration of dietary intake, timing, and individual health needs. Here are some foundational guidelines to assist in this integration:

Starting with one dietary strategy before incorporating the other can often be beneficial. For many, beginning with the ketogenic diet may be advisable as it requires significant changes to one's macronutrient ratios. Establishing a routine on the ketogenic diet first allows the body to adjust to fat as a primary energy source. Once this has been established, intermittent fasting can be introduced gradually to enhance the effects of ketosis.

During eating periods, it is crucial to ensure that nutritional intake supports both ketosis and fasting. This means consuming adequate amounts of fats and proteins while keeping carbohydrate intake very low to maintain the state of ketosis. It's also important to focus on the quality of the foods consumed—choosing high-quality, nutrient-dense foods can help maintain health and energy levels.

Hydration and electrolyte balance are important in both diets but become critical when combined. Fasting and carbohydrate restriction can both lead to reductions in insulin levels, which can cause the kidneys to excrete more sodium and water. Supplementing with sodium, potassium, and magnesium can help maintain electrolyte balance and prevent symptoms such as fatigue, headaches, and muscle cramps.

It's critical to pay attention to your body and be willing to adjust your approach as needed. Combining fasting with a ketogenic diet can be challenging, and individual responses can vary significantly. Monitoring how you feel and seeking professional guidance to tailor the approach can ensure that it remains safe and effective.

Combining intermittent fasting with the ketogenic diet can enhance the benefits of both strategies, leading to improved fat loss, better metabolic health, and increased longevity. However, this combination should be approached with careful planning and consideration of individual health conditions to ensure it is done safely and effectively.

Fasting Mimicking Diets

Fasting-mimicking diets (FMD) is a novel nutritional concept designed to reap the benefits of fasting while still providing the body with food to minimize the stress and difficulties associated with traditional fasting methods. This dietary approach involves reducing calorie intake significantly for a set period to induce metabolic effects similar to those achieved through water-only fasting. This chapter explores the concept and execution of fasting-mimicking diets and discusses appropriate situations for their consideration.

Concept and Execution

The fasting-mimicking diet was developed based on the principle that you can trick the body into a fasting state by eating a specific composition of macronutrients—low in proteins and carbohydrates but relatively high in good fats. This approach aims to provide enough nutrients to sustain basic health, yet few enough to provoke the beneficial stress response associated with traditional fasting.

Design of the Diet

A typical fasting-mimicking diet lasts for about five days, a period considered sufficient to enhance the benefits of fasting without the harsh challenges of longer fasts. During these five days, calorie intake is usually restricted to about 40-50% of an individual's normal daily calorie requirement. The specific nutrient composition focuses on the following:

High Fats: Approximately 50-60% of the total calories come from healthy fats like nuts, seeds, and olive oil. These help to sustain energy levels and hormone production without spiking insulin and glucose levels.

Low Proteins: Protein intake is significantly reduced to about 10% of the daily calories. Lowering protein intake is crucial for reducing the activation of certain pathways, such as motor, which are associated with ageing and cancer.

Low Carbohydrates: Carbohydrates are limited to about 30-40% of the total calorie intake and are sourced from complex carbs like vegetables and whole grains, which have a minimal impact on blood sugar levels.

Daily Routine:

Participants consume specially formulated meals that adhere to these macronutrient ratios. The meals are typically prepared and packaged as ready-to-eat servings that include plant-based energy bars, soups, a variety of snacks, and drinks, which are calibrated to ensure nutrient balance and satiety.

When to Consider a Fasting Mimicking Diet

The fasting-mimicking diet is particularly suitable in several scenarios due to its unique blend of providing nourishment and inducing physiological fasting responses:

For Those New to Fasting:

Individuals interested in fasting but concerned about the physical and psychological challenges of traditional methods may find fasting-mimicking diets a more feasible option. The FMD provides a gentle introduction to the benefits of fasting without complete abstinence from food, making the transition easier and often more sustainable.

Individuals with Health Restrictions:

People who have certain health conditions that make traditional fasting unsafe—such as diabetes, low blood pressure, or those taking specific medications—might be able to use FMD as a safer alternative. However, it is crucial to undertake this diet under medical supervision to adjust any medications and monitor health responses during the diet.

Aging and Longevity:

Research suggests that FMD can promote longevity and reduce the risk of age-related diseases. This is likely due to its effects on biomarkers associated with ageing, such as inflammation, insulin resistance, and hormone levels regulating growth and reproduction.

Chronic Disease Management:

There is emerging evidence that FMD may help manage chronic diseases, including autoimmune diseases and diabetes. By reducing inflammatory markers and improving metabolic flexibility, FMD can play a role in managing disease severity and improving overall health outcomes.

Fasting-mimicking diets offer a novel approach to traditional fasting by allowing individuals to eat while still activating the physiological and cellular benefits of a fasting state. This diet, particularly useful for those who find complete fasting too challenging or medically unsafe, must be planned carefully and preferably undertaken with professional guidance to maximize benefits and ensure health safety. As with any dietary intervention, personal circumstances and health conditions should guide the decision to start an FMD, ensuring it complements one's health goals and lifestyle needs effectively.

Troubleshooting Common Issues

Integrating fasting into your lifestyle effectively often involves navigating through common pitfalls and obstacles that can arise. Whether you are new to fasting or have encountered plateaus or setbacks in your ongoing fasting regimen, refining your approach is crucial. This chapter provides insights on how to refine your fasting strategies and includes expert tips to enhance the effectiveness and sustainability of your fasting plan.

Refining Your Approach

The effectiveness of fasting can often be hindered by issues such as choosing an inappropriate fasting window, mismanaging caloric intake during eating windows, or neglecting hydration and electrolyte balance. To overcome these issues, a thoughtful reassessment of your fasting plan is necessary.

Reevaluate your fasting window. The window should fit into your daily schedule while maximizing the metabolic benefits of fasting. If you find adherence challenging or if the benefits have plateaued, consider adjusting the length of the fast. Shortening or lengthening your fasting window can help align the regimen more closely with your lifestyle and biological needs.

Examine your caloric intake during eating periods. It is crucial to avoid overeating and to focus on nutrient-dense foods that provide sufficient fibre, protein, and healthy fats. This ensures that you are not only maintaining a caloric deficit but also receiving adequate nutrition. Mismanagement here can lead to poor results and diminished health benefits.

Maintain adequate hydration and electrolyte balance. Fasting can lead to dehydration and mineral imbalances, particularly during extended or water-only fasts. Increasing your intake of water and electrolyte-rich foods or supplements can prevent common symptoms like headaches, fatigue, and irritability.

If you are new to fasting or considering more stringent methods, such as prolonged fasting or fasting-mitigating diets, start gradually. A progressive approach allows your body to adapt without undue stress, making the transition smoother and more sustainable over the long term.

Expert Tips and Tricks

Enhancing your fasting regimen involves more than just tweaking its components; it also includes adopting practices that facilitate a deeper integration of fasting into your lifestyle.

One pivotal practice is maintaining consistent timing for your fasting periods. Aligning your fasting window to occur at the same times each day can help regulate your body's circadian rhythms, potentially making the fasting process feel more natural and minimizing side effects like sleep disturbances and daytime fatigue.

Incorporating mindful eating practices during your eating windows can also profoundly impact the success of your fasting regimen. This includes being attentive to the speed at which you eat, the composition of your meals, and the satiety signals your body sends. Eating slowly and deliberately helps enhance digestion and absorption of nutrients, ensuring that you are truly nourishing your body and not just filling it.

Strategic use of caffeinated beverages like coffee and tea during the fasting period can also be beneficial. These beverages can help suppress appetite and provide a mental boost without breaking the fast, as long as they are consumed without added sugars or milk.

However, it is important to moderate caffeine intake to avoid sleep disturbances.

Integrating regular physical activity, particularly just before breaking your fast, can enhance the fat-burning potential of fasting. Exercise during the fasting state can increase insulin sensitivity and accelerate the depletion of glycogen stores, leading directly to increased fat oxidation.

Successfully navigating the challenges of fasting involves a combination of well-thought-out adjustments to your fasting plan and the adoption of practices that complement the biological and psychological demands of fasting. By carefully refining your approach and incorporating these expert tips, you can enhance both the effectiveness and the enjoyment of your fasting experience, leading to sustained health benefits and a more adaptable lifestyle adjustment.

CHAPTER 9

SUSTAINING YOUR NEW LIFESTYLE

Adopting intermittent fasting is not merely a dietary change but a lifestyle transformation. Sustaining this lifestyle over the long term requires more than willpower; it involves strategic adaptations and integrating fasting into your personal and social identity. This chapter explores how to maintain intermittent fasting as a long-term practice, including adjusting the approach as you age and making fasting an integral part of your lifestyle.

Maintaining Intermittent Fasting Long-Term

Adapting as You Age

As the body ages, its nutritional needs, metabolism, and overall health status change, necessitating crucial adjustments to any fasting regimen. What might have been effective during the younger years could be less so later in life. For example, the body's ability to recover from stress or its metabolic rate can decrease with age, and the risk for various age-related diseases increases. It's vital to adapt your fasting schedule to these changes.

Consider the intensity and frequency of fasting sessions. Older adults may find it beneficial to shorten fasting periods or reduce the frequency of extended fasts to prevent muscle loss and maintain energy levels. Nutrition during eating windows should focus more on high-quality proteins, essential fats, and micronutrients to support muscle maintenance, cognitive function, and cellular health.

It's essential for older adults to monitor their physiological responses closely. Fasting can have a more significant impact on blood sugar levels, hydration status, and overall energy levels in older adults. Regular consultations with healthcare providers to assess health markers and adapt fasting protocols are advisable to ensure that the practice remains beneficial and safe.

Making Fasting a Part of Your Identity

Integrating intermittent fasting into your identity involves seeing it not just as something you do, but as a part of who you are. This integration is key to sustaining the practice through social pressures, lifestyle changes, and personal challenges.

One effective strategy is to align fasting with your broader health and life goals. Whether you're focused on longevity, managing a health condition, or improving mental clarity, view fasting as a tool that actively helps you achieve these goals. This perspective helps to reinforce why you are fasting, making it a core part of your health regimen.

Next, build a community or join existing groups of like-minded individuals who practice intermittent fasting. Sharing experiences and challenges with peers can provide emotional support, enhance motivation, and deepen your commitment to fasting. This community aspect can transform fasting from a solitary endeavor into a social practice, enriching the experience and integrating it into your social identity.

Educate those around you about the benefits and reasons behind your choice to fast. This can facilitate social acceptance and might even inspire others, further reinforcing your identity as someone who values and practices intentional eating for health.

Celebrate your fasting achievements, no matter how small. Acknowledging milestones not only boosts your morale but also solidifies fasting as a key component of your lifestyle. Whether it's improved health metrics, weight loss, or simply sticking to a fasting schedule, each success is a step toward making fasting a permanent part of your life.

Continued Learning and Adaptation

Integrating intermittent fasting into your lifestyle is a dynamic process that benefits greatly from ongoing learning and adaptation. As nutritional science and health research evolve, so too should your fasting strategies. This chapter discusses the importance of staying informed about the latest scientific developments and adjusting your approach to fasting as new insights become available.

Staying Informed with Latest Research

Keeping abreast of the latest research is crucial for anyone committed to maintaining an effective and safe fasting regimen. The world of nutritional science is rapidly advancing, with new studies frequently challenging old paradigms and suggesting more refined approaches to fasting.

Engaging with a variety of professional and academic resources is essential to remaining updated. Regular interaction with healthcare professionals who specialize in diet and nutrition, such as dietitians and nutritionists, can provide personalized insights and recommendations that consider the latest research findings. These professionals can help interpret complex studies and suggest practical applications to enhance the effectiveness of your fasting plan.

Academic journals are primary sources of new research data and findings. Subscribing to or regularly reviewing journals focused on clinical nutrition and metabolism offers direct access to new research that could influence fasting practices. Additionally, health and wellness media—including reputable blogs, podcasts, and websites—often discuss new research in a more accessible format, helping to distil complex information into actionable advice.

Participating in conferences and seminars on nutrition and health also plays a vital role in staying informed. These gatherings are not only about the dissemination of new research but also provide opportunities to ask questions directly to experts, participate in discussions, and network with peers who share similar interests in health and fasting.

Evolving with Scientific Insights

Adapting your fasting strategy in response to new scientific insights ensures that your practices remain aligned with the best available evidence, optimizing health benefits and minimizing risks.

The key to successful adaptation is flexibility. Be willing to modify various aspects of your fasting regimen—including the timing, duration, and frequency of fasts—based on new evidence. For instance, if emerging research suggests that a different fasting interval is more beneficial for metabolic health or weight management, experimenting with this new timing could prove advantageous.

Personal experimentation, guided by professional advice and reliable data, can help tailor fasting practices to your specific needs. Utilizing health tracking devices or regular medical checkups can provide quantitative feedback on how adjustments to your fasting regimen affect your health. This data-driven approach allows for refined and personalized fasting strategies that are responsive to both scientific research and personal health metrics.

Consider fasting as part of a broader holistic health strategy. Integrating fasting with other health-promoting practices such as balanced nutrition, regular physical activity, and effective stress management can amplify the benefits and mitigate potential drawbacks. This integrated approach not only improves overall health outcomes but also aligns with a sustainable and adaptable lifestyle.

Maintaining an intermittent fasting lifestyle over the long term requires more than just discipline; it necessitates a commitment to continuous learning and flexibility to adapt to new scientific findings. By staying informed through various credible sources and being willing to adjust your fasting practices based on personal experiences and new research, you can ensure that your fasting regimen remains beneficial, safe, and tailored to your evolving health needs. This proactive approach to learning and adaptation is essential for anyone looking to sustain intermittent fasting as a lifelong health practice.

Integrating Mindfulness and Meditation

Integrating mindfulness and meditation into an intermittent fasting regimen can significantly enhance the mental health benefits of fasting. These practices help in managing the psychological challenges associated with fasting, such as mood fluctuations and feelings of deprivation. Additionally, mindfulness and meditation can improve overall emotional resilience, making it easier to adhere to fasting protocols and lifestyle changes. This chapter explores how these techniques can be effectively combined with fasting to support both mental and physical health.

Enhancing Mental Health Benefits

Mindfulness and meditation are well-documented for their benefits in reducing stress, anxiety, and depression and improving cognitive function. These practices involve a heightened state of awareness and focused attention, which can be particularly beneficial for individuals engaged in fasting. By fostering a mindful approach to eating and hunger, individuals can experience a more harmonious relationship with food and their bodies.

The practice of mindfulness during fasting helps to cultivate a non-judgmental awareness of the body's hunger cues and emotional states. This awareness is crucial in distinguishing between true physical hunger and emotional eating triggers, such as stress or boredom, which can often sabotage fasting and dietary goals. Moreover, mindfulness enhances the appreciation of food, which can make meals more satisfying, even when they are less frequent or smaller in quantity due to fasting schedules.

Meditation supports fasting by improving stress resilience. Stress is a common reason for people to abandon fasting, as it can lead to overeating and a preference for high-calorie, nutrient-poor foods that provide temporary comfort. Regular meditation lowers stress levels, thereby helping individuals maintain consistency in their fasting regimen and make healthier food choices during eating windows.

Techniques That Complement Fasting

Several specific mindfulness and meditation techniques can be particularly useful for individuals practising intermittent fasting. One effective method iseating with awarenessIt entails giving the act of eating its entire focusand drinking. During eating windows, individuals are encouraged to eat slowly and without distraction, savour each bite, and be fully present with the flavours, textures, and smells of their food. This practice not only enhances satisfaction and enjoyment from meals but also promotes better digestion and satiety, which are beneficial for weight management and metabolic health.

Body scan meditations are also beneficial as they involve mentally scanning through different parts of the body to identify areas of tension or discomfort. This technique can be used to navigate the physical sensations of hunger during fasting periods, helping individuals differentiate between true hunger and habitual eating impulses. Recognizing these signals can empower individuals to respond to their body's needs more thoughtfully, enhancing the effectiveness of the fasting process.

Additionally, incorporating daily sessions of guided imagery or visualization can reinforce fasting goals and outcomes. Visualizing the positive health outcomes of fasting, such as improved energy levels, weight loss, or better metabolic health, can boost motivation and commitment to the fasting process.

Integrating meditation practices such as Transcendental Meditation or mindfulness-based stress reduction (MBSR) into daily routines can also provide robust stress management tools that support the mental demands of fasting. These practices offer structured ways to reduce stress and anxiety, improve mental clarity, and enhance overall emotional well-being.

Mindfulness and meditation are powerful tools that can significantly enhance the mental health benefits of intermittent fasting. By promoting a mindful relationship with food, improving stress resilience, and enhancing emotional awareness, these practices support individuals in not only adhering to fasting schedules but also in achieving their broader health and wellness goals. Integrating these techniques into a fasting regimen ensures a holistic approach to health that benefits the mind as much as the body, making fasting a more effective and sustainable lifestyle choice.

Fasting and Global Traditions

Fasting is a practice deeply embedded in the cultural fabric of societies around the world. It has been utilized for millennia, not only for its health benefits but also for spiritual, religious, and traditional reasons. This chapter explores how integrating the wisdom from global fasting traditions can enhance and inform modern fasting practices, providing a richer, more culturally informed perspective on this transformative health strategy.

Integrating Cultural Wisdom

The practice of fasting is ancient and universal, transcending modern dietary trends to include a vast array of cultural and spiritual dimensions. Many cultures view fasting as a means to cleanse both the body and the spirit, a practice that is often integrated into ceremonial and ritual contexts. This traditional wisdom can provide valuable insights into the holistic benefits of fasting, encouraging a more comprehensive approach that considers the mental, spiritual, and physical aspects of health.

In many traditions, fasting is not merely about abstaining from food but involves a period of reflection, prayer, or meditation. These practices suggest that the benefits of fasting may be enhanced when combined with mindfulness and contemplative activities that promote mental and spiritual health. This holistic approach can offer modern fasters a way to incorporate these spiritual and reflective practices into their fasting regimens, potentially increasing the practice's overall efficacy and sustainability.

Traditional fasting practices often include specific rituals for entering and breaking fasts, which emphasize respect for the body's needs and the sacred nature of food. These rituals can teach modern practitioners to approach fasting with a greater sense of reverence and gratitude, perspectives often absent in purely clinical or weight-loss-focused fasting protocols.

Fasting Practices Around the World

Fasting practices vary significantly across different cultures and religions, each adding a unique flavor to the fasting experience and offering diverse insights into how fasting can be practiced effectively:

Islamic Ramadan: Perhaps one of the most well-known fasting practices globally, Ramadan involves a month of fasting from sunrise to sunset. The fast includes abstention from all food and drink during daylight hours. The breaking of the fast, called Iftar, is a communal meal that begins with the eating of date and water, a practice said to balance blood sugar levels quickly and hydrate the body efficiently.

Hindu Fasting: Hinduism incorporates various fasting practices, often linked to religious festivals and lunar cycles. Fasts may be partial or complete, and the consumption of fruits or specific foods might be allowed. The practice emphasizes self-discipline and spiritual growth, showing a path to fasting where the focus is as much on mental purity as on physical health.

Biblical Fasting: In Christianity, particularly within Eastern Orthodox communities, fasting is a significant religious undertaking. Periods like Lent involve abstaining from meat and dairy products to purify the body and spirit. This practice underlines the importance of moderation and the avoidance of indulgence, principles that can be adapted for health-focused fasting.

Buddhist Fasting: Buddhist monks traditionally do not eat after noon. By limiting the time window during which food is consumed, this practice helps regulate the body's health and is seen as a means to improve meditation and focus.

Fasting is a versatile and adaptive practice that has been shaped by thousands of years of cultural traditions. By incorporating cultural wisdom and varied practices from around the world, modern fasting regimens can be enriched and deepened. This global perspective not only enhances the physical health benefits of fasting but also integrates spiritual, mental, and communal dimensions, making fasting a more holistic and transformative practice. Whether adopted for health, spiritual purification, or as part of cultural practice, fasting remains a powerful tool for improving well-being and connecting with a broader human tradition.

Looking Ahead

As you progress in your journey with intermittent fasting, it becomes crucial to continually set new goals and explore broader aspects of health and wellness. This chapter discusses how to expand your health horizons and continuously evolve the goals that guide your fasting and overall health strategy. This forward-thinking approach not only helps sustain motivation but also ensures that the benefits of fasting grow and adapt to your changing lifestyle needs.

Setting New Goals

The practice of setting goals is fundamental in maintaining the momentum and efficacy of intermittent fasting over time. Initially, goals often center on weight loss or managing a specific health issue. However, as these initial goals are met, it's important to reassess and set new objectives to continue progressing.

Expanding your goals involves several considerations. First, reflect on what you've achieved thus far and what aspects of your health and wellness could still improve. Consider setting goals that not only challenge you but also enhance your quality of life. These include improving physical performance, enhancing mental clarity, achieving greater emotional stability, or even exploring new dietary practices that complement intermittent fasting.

- Another approach is to set process-oriented goals instead of outcome-oriented ones. For example, rather than aiming to lose a certain amount of weight, you might set a goal to adhere to your fasting schedule more consistently or integrate mindfulness practices into your daily routine to enhance the mental health benefits of fasting.

Expanding Your Health Horizons

As you become more accustomed to the practice of fasting, it opens the door to exploring broader health concepts and integrating other wellness practices that can synergize with intermittent fasting. Expanding your health horizons means looking beyond the basics and understanding how different aspects of lifestyle, nutrition, and mental health interconnect.

One way to expand your health horizons is through the integration of physical activities that align with your fasting schedule. Activities such as yoga, Pilates, or even more dynamic exercises like HIIT (high-intensity interval training) can complement your fasting protocol, optimizing energy use and enhancing metabolic health.

Exploring other dietary approaches that focus on nutrition quality, such as the Mediterranean diet or plant-based eating, can provide complementary benefits to fasting. These diets emphasize whole foods, fruits, vegetables, and healthy fats, which can help improve the overall quality of your diet during eating windows, leading to better health outcomes.

Mental health is another critical area that often benefits from fasting's mindful nature. Engaging more deeply with practices that promote mental well-being, such as meditation, deep breathing exercises, and stress management techniques, can improve not only your fasting experience but also your overall life satisfaction and emotional resilience.

Looking ahead in your fasting journey involves continuously setting new goals and expanding your understanding of health and wellness. By embracing a broader perspective on what it means to be healthy, integrating complementary practices, and setting progressively challenging goals, you can enhance the benefits of intermittent fasting. This holistic approach ensures that fasting remains a rewarding and health-promoting part of your lifestyle, adaptable to your evolving personal and health needs. Embrace the journey of exploration and growth, and let your fasting practice be a gateway to greater health and well-being.

Appendix

Glossary of Terms

Frequently Asked Questions

Resource Directory

Books, websites, and more

Acknowledgements

Contributors

Special Thanks

About the Author

Author's Biography

Background in nutrition and health coaching

Bibliography

References

Further Reading

This expanded structure not only ensures a comprehensive coverage of intermittent fasting specifically tailored for women over 50, but also provides practical advice, varied recipes, and motivational stories to engage and inspire your readers throughout their journey. This approach will make the eBook a valuable and enduring resource.

www.ingramcontent.com/pod-product-compliance
Lightning Source LLC
Chambersburg PA
CBHW070849050426
42453CB00012B/2097